DESTINED TO BE: WALKING INTO YOUR GOD GIVEN DESTINY ONE STEP AT A TIME

DANYELLE SCROGGINS

ALSO BY DANYELLE SCROGGINS

Non Fiction

Not Until You're Ready

His Mistress or God's Daughter

Processed For Purpose

40 Days of Healing Journal

Fiction Books

Destiny's Decision

Put It In Ink

The Power Series:

Pain, Restoration, Love, & Forgiving *Series*

Unless otherwise indicated, Scriptures verses are from the taken King James Version of the Bible.

"Scripture quotations are taken from the New American Standard Bible®, Copyright © 1960, 1962, 1963, 1968, 1971, 1972, 1973, 1975, 1977, 1995 by The Lockman Foundation

Used by permission." (www.Lockman.org)

Published by:

Divinely Sown Publishing

DESTINED TO BE: Walking Into Your God Given Destiny One Step At A Time

Copyright © 2024 Unless otherwise indicated, Scriptures verses are from the taken King James Version of the Bible.

All Rights Reserved. Printed in the United States of America. No part of this book may be used or reproduced in any manner whatsoever without written permission except in the case of brief quotations embodied in critical articles and reviews.

Special discounts are available for quantity purchases. For details contact the publisher at the address above.

First Edition paperback 2024

Printed in the United States of America.

Cover Designed by Danyelle Scroggins

Dedicated to

Those who have been wasting time trying to figure out the alternatives instead of embracing the assignment.
Pastor Danyelle

A WORD FROM THE AUTHOR

Dear Reader,

Thank you for picking up this book and beginning a journey with me through the winding paths of life. Writing it has been a joy, a labor of love that stands as a testament to the trials, triumphs, and revelations that have shaped my walk with God.

In sharing these stories and testimonies, my hope is to inspire and encourage you to embrace your journey with a renewed sense of purpose. Life's challenges aren't meant to break us but to refine us, to draw us closer to God, and to reveal the strength and resilience He has woven into our spirits. As you turn these pages, I pray you feel empowered to discover your unique purpose and the sacred assignment waiting to be awakened within you.

This book is more than a collection of experiences; it's a call to lift your gaze beyond daily routines, to see the extraordinary plans God has prepared just for you. Each chapter is a reminder that you were created with intention. Through faith and perseverance, we can walk boldly in our true calling, emerging victorious as we align ourselves with His design.

I encourage you buy the companion **Study Guide** and to let these words resonate in your heart, to reflect deeply on your own journey, and to step forward in faith toward the life God has crafted for you. In our shared experiences, we find the strength to press on, the wisdom to grow, and the faith to believe in God's promises.

May this book be a wellspring of hope and encouragement and a catalyst for a closer connection with the One who has PURPOSED you for greatness. Remember, every person has their own journey, and by sharing our experiences, we bless and uplift those who may be struggling to understand their own path.

Blessings,

Pastor Danyelle Scroggins

"For I know the plans that I have for you,' declares the Lord, 'plans for prosperity and not for disaster, to give you a future and a hope."

Jeremiah 29:11

ABOUT DESTINED TO BE: WALKING INTO YOUR DESTINY ONE STEP AT A TIME

Destined To Be by Danyelle Scroggins is a powerful, faith-filled book that urges readers to stop wasting time on distractions and alternatives and instead embrace the unique purpose God has assigned them. Scroggins emphasizes that each person has a divine calling crafted by God to align with their talents and experiences. However, many people get sidetracked by fear, doubt, and the temptation to follow easier or more appealing paths.

Through personal stories, biblical insights, and practical advice, *Destined To Be* challenges readers to break free from indecision, fear, and procrastination. Scroggins reminds readers that waiting for the "perfect time" or looking for other options often leads to frustration and an unfulfilled life. Instead, she encourages believers to trust God's timing and step into their calling with faith, knowing they have already been equipped for success.

A key message in the book is the danger of comparison and procrastination. Scroggins warns that focusing on others' success or waiting for ideal conditions can derail one's divine purpose. She offers practical steps for discerning your God-given assignment, eliminating distractions, and surrounding yourself with supportive, godly relationships.

At its core, *Destined To Be* is a call to action. Scroggins urges readers to take ownership of their calling, reminding them that God qualifies those He calls. By embracing their purpose and stepping out in faith, readers can live a life of fulfillment and divine alignment. The book is a spiritual guide and a motivational roadmap for anyone ready to stop wasting time and start living out their God-ordained destiny.

PROLOGUE

Training wasn't bad for me. I was used to running and fighting with boy cousins. Curtis, Quentin, Patrick, and even my first boyfriend Ray had all made me tough. They wrestled me as if I were a boy, and I fought back like a girl who refused to give up. So, instead of my broad shoulder, thick traps, and wide back being an unattractive curse, they turned into what I'd used to later get through every rough or tough occurrence; my blessing.

I fought the urge to do something I'd heard men forever say, women can't do. They said, "God won't do," and that is, call a woman to preach. The tumbling of my belly when someone was preaching. The ache in my heart every single time I heard, "God is not calling no woman to preach."

The private bathtub moments when whomever was on the phone line turn into my audience. The friends' calls that turned into an all-out pastoral counseling session. The desire to sit under anyone's feet who would take the time to teach me the oracles of

God. All moments that made me dread the truth of my assignment. While at the same time, solidifying the obvious that I and others were trying to cover up.

Then I had an epiphany.

If preaching is serving and protecting the bodies of men by keeping them from fire, and serving others was my calling, then I'd just join the Shreveport Fire Department and do both: serve and protect the bodies of others and keep men from fire.

Heck yeah! I had it all under control.

I trained for six months. Running, jogging, lifting, studying and doing everything that would help me past the firefighters agility test. After passing the paperwork, the real test came: the physical challenge.

The day had finally arrived.

I ran with the hose, maneuvering it into place. I carried a 350-pound dummy up and down the stairs. I had done it. I was almost there—just one last task. Hook up three sections of the fire hose to prove I was strong enough for the job.

The sun was warm, not too hot, just perfect. The day was already going well, and I could practically see my future laid out before me. A good-paying job, serving God's people, four days off at a time, and coworkers who would become like family. Time to work in the beauty shop on my off days, saving up for the life I'd always wanted. All of it was falling into place.

But all...pieces to my plan.

I got down to the last task, feeling good about myself. My uncle's sister, Lisa, was there, cheering me on. Sometimes, a little support is all you need to push through.

I won't lie, I was a tired boss. Legs, arms, everything feeling like jelly. Still, I was determined.

I bent down and connected the first piece of the hose.

"She did it!" I say to myself.

I closed my eyes, praying for the strength to get through the next one.

As if the skies had opened, I heard a voice, clear as day: "This is not the assignment, Danyelle."

I shook my head, trying to silence it. *This is the way. There is no other way.* I connected the second piece. The last few pieces were in my view.

You got this Gatlin. It's yours.

But the voice came again, louder this time: "This is not what I told you to do."

I fought back: "I can't preach. This will have to do."

Suddenly, my legs started cramping—bad. It felt like all the blood and energy drained from my body, leaving me frozen. Time was running out.

I heard Chief Crawford tell Lisa, "If she finishes, she's in."

Then God spoke again: "If you love Me, keep My commandment."

One tear slid down my cheek. "I quit," I whispered.

Lisa urged me, "Don't stop! He's going to let you in! Are you sure you want to quit?"

I shook my head. In that moment, I knew: pleasing myself and her (because she wanted for me what I wanted), would mean disappointing the One who loved me first.

I stood up from the hose, closed my eyes, and when I opened them, I walked away.

There was no pretending anymore.

I wasn't meant to be a firefighter—at least not in the way I thought. Maybe honorary, but my calling was different. I wasn't here to fight earthly fires. I was called to extinguish spiritual ones. Called to protect the souls of the saints so they would never burn in eternity. Called to blow out the flames of destruction so those who heard me could make a choice—to choose whom they would serve.

Called to a purpose higher than those who fight fire, are the ones who keep you from living eternally in fire.

With a deep breath and a heart full of resolve, I started my car and drove away from the fire training camp on Greenwood Road. I headed back to my house on Cooper Road with a fresh testimony in my heart: no matter how many substitutes you come up with, nothing will ever replace what you were truly ordained to do.

When you finally accept that, the path may not be easy, but the burden will lift. Because the easiest thing to accomplish is what you were Destined To Be.

Let's Pray:

Father, I lift up the one reading this book. I pray that the transformative message and language of my heart will usher them into a sweet revelation of You, Your plan, and Your will for them on earth. Speak to their hearts and minds and give them the sweet relief they need in order to finish the journey as You desire. In the powerful, mighty, wonderful, and awesome name of Jesus, I pray. Amen.

CHAPTER 1
TAGGED BY HEAVEN

Close your eyes and let your spirit paint this scene with me.

For nine long months, Cassandra Goodman has carried the life of a child within her womb. From a tiny, embryonic seed, this life has matured into a fully formed baby, ready to embark on its divine mission on Earth. As if under the guidance of a master director, the contractions begin—a signal that the time has come.

At first, the contractions are mild, spaced ten minutes apart. But as the baby prepares to descend, they quicken and intensify. Each contraction is a wave, pushing the child closer to its earthly assignment. Then, with one final command to push, Cassandra gives it everything she has, her body bowing to the will of creation, defying gravity itself. Her muscles tighten and release. Someone is calling the baby to leave its safe haven inside the womb. Everything that's held the baby secure for nine months begins to detach, except for one final connection—the umbilical cord. And at last, the baby breaches the threshold between heaven and earth, as though sent by God on a mission.

Before the baby is washed, held, or even comforted, the neonatal nurse steps forward with a tag, carefully placing it around the baby's tiny wrist. This tag is more than just a label. It holds the baby's last name, weight, gender, and the exact time of birth. In this moment, the baby is no longer just a part of the mother—it has been given an identity of its own. The tag ties the baby to where it came from, its entrance into this world, and even its physical attributes. Though the father may be standing by, in awe or even tears, the mother is given full recognition for this act of life. Only when the father signs his name to the birth certificate does he share in this moment, giving the baby his last name.

All the credit for this new life is assigned to the mother, despite the fact that she didn't create the seed. She was the vessel, the holding cell, nurturing the seed until it was ready to live independently of her.

Who but God could orchestrate something so miraculous?

But let's go deeper.

In Jeremiah 1:5, God reveals something profound to the prophet: "Before I formed you in the womb, I knew you. Before you were born, I sanctified you; I ordained you a prophet to the nations." Most scholars agree this verse highlights God's predestination of Jeremiah's life. But there's more to uncover.

One Sunday, while I was preaching, something extraordinary happened. God interrupted my message with a vision, a fresh revelation that left me awestruck. In this vision, He slipped a band around my arm, a tag, and I realized He was holding a string connected to it. In that moment, I could have broken into an old-time Baptist shout right there at the pulpit.

For the first time, God showed me that the neonatal nurse isn't the only one tagging babies when they arrive on earth. He revealed that *we are tagged by heaven itself*, and He is the one holding the string.

It gets even deeper.

God showed me that the further away we are from Him, the easier it is for our tag, our string, to get caught in the snares of this world—trapped by ungodly things, tangled up in confusion, or even torn away. But when we stay close to Him, the line remains clear. We hear His voice more clearly, and our path remains untangled, straight, and connected to His divine purpose.

Then He brought me right back to Jeremiah 1:5. In real time, during that sermon, the Lord revealed that we are tagged by heaven. Before we were placed in the wombs of our mothers, before we were even the seed in our daddy, God already knew us. He had already sanctified us and ordained us for our specific journey.

In other words, you have been *tagged* by heaven.

Your arrival on this earth was no accident. You weren't born out of mere fleshly desires or human error. You were brought to this realm with your destiny intact. No matter how chaotic or flawed the circumstances of your birth may have been, your purpose was already sealed by God.

You have the power to rise above the circumstances of your birth, the method of your arrival, and the challenges of your past. All you need to do is reconnect with the One who tagged you; the One who assigned you this life.

Each and every one of us has been chosen, tagged, and assigned for a divine purpose.

But, how many of us are still searching for that assignment? How many of us live our lives, tethered to God by a string that's been tangled and knotted by the chaos of this world, unaware of the greater calling that's been placed on our lives?

It's not by coincidence that we are born into specific circumstances. Just like a child is not randomly born into a hospital or under the care of any nurse—there's an intentionality behind every detail. The very weight of the baby, the time of its birth, and the circumstances surrounding its arrival all contribute to a grander story—a story that began long before the mother felt her first contraction.

There's a purpose to the timing. There's a reason for the weight you carry.

Let's think about this for a moment. A newborn baby, minutes after its arrival, is tagged. It's identified, weighed, and given a timestamp. The hospital knows exactly who this baby is, where it came from, and what it needs to thrive. In the same way, God has already tagged us before we ever breathed our first breath. Our weight, our timing, our journey is known to Him before we take our first step.

But unlike the earthly tag that fades with time, the tag from heaven remains with us. It's a divine marker, an identifier that seals us as chosen. We may not always see it, but that doesn't make it any less real.

This leads me to an important truth: each of us, no matter our background or what we've endured, has been intentionally placed here, on this earth, at this time. We are not here by chance or coincidence. We were not dropped into this world without purpose or direction. God has tagged us. We are known, sanctified, and *assigned*.

So the question becomes: are you ready to walk in the assignment that's been given to you?

For some of us, the weight of the world, the noise of our circumstances, has distracted us from hearing the voice of the One who tagged us. We've forgotten the string that connects us to Him, letting it slip through our fingers as we chase after lesser things. But just as a newborn baby is cared for and nurtured, God is waiting to realign us with our purpose. He's waiting to remind us of the tag we've carried since before we were formed.

And that's why, no matter where you are in life right now, no matter how far you may feel from your assignment, it's not too late to remember:

You've been tagged.

You've been tagged by God.

You've been chosen.

You've been assigned.

And, you've been given a mission to fulfill.

CHAPTER 2
CHOSEN & ASSIGNED

Yes, it may sound impossible—this idea of being chosen for a specific purpose. But whether or not you've ever stopped to consider the supernatural within the natural, the truth remains: nothing God has ever created came into existence without blueprints from the Master Planner.

God's creations aren't random or haphazard. Every single thing that was and is has been designed to fulfill a role within His grand plan. And that includes you and me. Our creation is more intricate, more intentional, and more profound than any human mind could fully grasp. Even the most dynamic, awe-inspiring movie or work of art could only ever scratch the surface of the complexity behind our divine design.

Think about that for a moment. Every part of you—your strengths, your quirks, your passions, even the things you see as flaws—were woven together with a purpose. There's not a single element of your being that is accidental. Every moving piece, every fiber of your existence, has been predetermined and laid out to fit perfectly within God's purpose for your life. But here's the key: this divine blueprint doesn't fully reveal itself until you draw closer to Him.

As you seek Him, the design becomes clearer. The more you press into His presence, the more you begin to understand why you're here, what you were made for, and how you can walk in it. Oh, wheee… it may seem like a lot to take in, but in its simplest form: *You were created with a specific purpose, and the closer you get to God, the more that purpose is revealed.*

I promise you, what seems so hard to grasp is actually so simple once you realize it.

Let's break it down—look at something as basic as math. Before you're introduced to numbers and equations, even as a baby, you instinctively understand that if you have something in each hand, you feel better, more fulfilled. One puff chip? Not enough. Two? Ah, now there's balance, right? It's because your capacity to hold two was already within you, even before you understood the concept of numbers.

And if you're anything like my grandbaby, before she could even count, she'd stretch out her little hand and say, "Give me five." Now, she had no idea what *five* actually was, but somehow, it was embedded in her—this numeric capacity beyond what she had yet learned. The funny thing was, she always asked for *five*, whether it was five dollars or five pieces of candy. She skipped right past asking for one or two and went straight for five, like it was her natural request.

So what did we do? We started counting with her. "One, two, three, four, five…" We taught her the numbers so she could understand the gravity of her request. But even without knowing what five was, she had this instinct, this drive to reach for more than what she could hold in her hands.

Now, I shared that with you to show this: whatever it is you've been chosen for, whatever you've been assigned to accomplish, is far beyond what you can fully grasp right now. It's bigger than your current capacity to hold. It stretches far beyond the environment you've grown up in or the limitations you think you have.

You were chosen to meet a need, and you've been assigned to fulfill the *capacity of your seed.*

Think of that seed inside you like a potential that has already been placed within you. A seed that contains everything you're capable of becoming, but that capacity is unlocked and expanded as you draw nearer to God. Just like a seed knows how to grow into a tree, but needs the right environment—soil, water, sunlight—you, too, will see that potential grow as you lean into His plan for your life.

You were designed for something specific. The purpose that God has placed in you is not arbitrary or generic—it's as unique as your fingerprints. There is a need in this world that *only you* can meet, a void that only *you* can fill. And here's the powerful truth: God has already equipped you with everything you need to meet that need. It may not look like much right now, but just like my grandbaby asking for five, even when she didn't fully understand the number—your spirit already knows what you're capable of. It's asking for things beyond your current understanding because it knows you're meant for more.

Here's the thing: the challenges and discomfort you face in life are not signs that you're off track. On the contrary, they're proof that you're being stretched to meet the full capacity of your assignment. You're being shaped and molded to grow into what God has already seen in you. That's why certain things in your life may seem too big to handle, too far beyond your reach—it's because they *are*. But not for long.

As you grow closer to God, your ability to handle those things expands. Your faith increases, your perspective shifts, and what once seemed impossible suddenly becomes the very thing you're called to do. You realize that the seed inside of you was planted with a purpose, and that purpose will come to fruition as you stay connected to the One who planted it.

No builder starts construction without blueprints. No artist paints without vision. And God—our Master Planner—crafted your life with specific, intricate details before you ever took your first breath. There are no accidents here. You were designed on purpose, for a purpose.

The more you embrace this truth, the more you'll see that the things that used to overwhelm you were never meant to. They were meant to *stretch* you, to *grow* you into the fullness of your assignment. Just like the baby with two hands reaching for more, your spirit knows that you were meant for abundance, for overflow, and for impact.

You are not here to live a life of mediocrity or to simply exist. You were chosen to fulfill a need that no one else can, and assigned a mission that only your life can complete.

So the next time you find yourself overwhelmed by the size of the task before you, remember this: *You were created for this.* You've been chosen, specifically, and you've been equipped with the seed to meet the capacity of the need.

You're not just *here*. You're *assigned*.

CHAPTER 3
THE STRUGGLE WAS & IS REAL

Remember the story I shared at the beginning of the book in the prologue? I need to tell you something: the struggle was real. This wasn't just some half-hearted attempt to escape doing what God had called me to do. No, this was deep-seated hurt that I had to wrestle with—soul-shaking battles that I had to overcome before I could fully embrace who I was, and who I am, in Him.

I vividly remember one of those pivotal moments. I went to a pastor I deeply respected—someone I loved like a real PawPaw. I poured my heart out to him, telling him about my struggles, my fears, and my concerns about stepping into ministry. He listened, taking in every word. But when he finally spoke, his words hit me like a ton of bricks: *"No, I don't believe God called a woman to do anything except be a missionary. But by all means, if you get big, tell them you came from me."*

Even now, I can't fully tell you whether that was a blessing or an insult. But one thing was crystal clear—I heard something that changed me: *I will get big one day*, and he knew it too. In that moment, I realized he'd unintentionally prophesied over my life. Despite his disbelief in my calling, I would rise, and he would get some of the credit for those early lessons—not because I wanted to give it to him, but because I learned so much under his leadership. No matter the hurt, I couldn't erase the good that came from my time there.

Fast forward about ten years after that conversation. That same pastor called me into his office. I sat across from him, feeling the weight of the past years lingering in the room. Without much explanation, he handed me his white robe. It was more than just a gift—it was a *release*. That simple gesture spoke volumes. For me, it was his way of saying, "You now have my permission to be who God has called you to be."

I was overwhelmed. I held back my tears until I got in the car with my husband, and then I broke. I cried like a two-year-old child who had been left at daycare for the first time. The release was so intense because, at that moment, I knew heaven had accounted this as the final push I needed to fully step into my calling. Not long after, the pastor passed away, but in those final days, he gave me something priceless—permission to walk in the fullness of my purpose.

But the story doesn't stop there.

It goes deeper.

It goes back to the countless Sundays I spent sitting in churches where I heard message after message, only to have any fire lit in my heart extinguished by pastors who stood up and said, *"God hasn't called any woman to preach."* Talk about brokenness. One voice would lift me up, telling me I could do great things, and then another would come along and tear me right back down.

And just when I thought I couldn't take any more of this tug-of-war, life delivered another blow. My husband made the decision to leave behind family and everything we knew, like Abraham being called to a land he'd never seen. The command to go was clear, but my heart was torn. Obedience was calling, but comfort was screaming for us to stay.

We visited three churches, each time thinking the same thing: *This isn't it.* There was always something—a feeling that it wasn't where we were meant to be. Either too much chaos, or too much compromise. We'd look at each other and know, without saying a word, that the search wasn't over.

Then, we walked into the next church. And the moment we stepped through the doors, the pastor stood up, looked directly at me, and said, *"When are you going to preach your first sermon, ma'am?"*

For the first time in my life, a man publicly acknowledged the calling I had been struggling with for years. Right there, in front of everyone, my struggle was spoken out loud. But get this—it didn't begin that day in the church.

No, it started much earlier, when I was sitting in the living room wearing peach-colored Daisy Dukes and a Guess jacket, face to face with one of the greatest COGIC Superintendents to ever walk this earth—Superintendent David Gatlin Sr.

He looked at me, a young woman who had no idea of the weight of her future, and said, *"Sit down, baby girl, let's talk."*

I respected him. He was my father-in-law at the time, and I knew his words carried power. *"Yes, sir,"* I replied, unsure of what to expect.

"When you start standing before the people, I want you to always wear a robe," he said.

My eyebrows furrowed in confusion. A robe? What on earth was he talking about? I had no plans to stand before anyone for any reason, let alone wear a robe.

But he didn't stop there. "Every man you stand before may not be saved. Your personality is too big, and he may see something that takes his mind off God. If you are in a robe, it will cause spirits to be quenched, and God will be glorified."

At the time, I didn't understand a single word of what he was saying. Mantles? Robes? I was more confused than I'd ever been. I turned to my husband afterward and asked, *"Is he getting senile?"* He just looked at me, dead serious, and said, *"My dad's a seer. Sometimes he sees things on people that they don't even understand."*

I laughed it off. I thought to myself, *There's no way I'll be wearing a robe unless I'm either a judge or in a choir,* neither of which seemed remotely likely. At the time, I couldn't hold a note to save my life, and I had already dropped out of high school, sidestepping any idea of becoming a judge. I had no clue that God had a divine assignment waiting for me.

But as time went on, the window of my understanding started to crack open. Even though I didn't like what I saw on the other side of that window, I couldn't un-see it. And so, I wasted years running from my calling, trying to drown out the voice of God by doing what *I* wanted to do.

But let me tell you something: running only delays the inevitable.

I ran from the mantle that had been spoken over me—not because I didn't believe it, but because I didn't *want* to believe it. I wasn't ready. The weight of that calling terrified me. I wasn't sure if I could live up to it. But here's the thing: God has a way of preparing us, even when we think we're not equipped, even when we feel unworthy or afraid. He uses the very things we want to avoid, the very things we're running from, to shape us into who we're destined to become. And when the time is right, He'll use people, circumstances, and even setbacks to remind you of the assignment He's already placed on your life. There's no escaping it —not forever.

Fast forward to that moment when the pastor asked me the question that shook me to my core: *"When are you going to preach your first sermon?"* It felt like a door I had been leaning on for years suddenly flew wide open. His words cut through all my hesitation, my doubts, and my fears. It was as if he had been sent by God to fast-track me into pastoral leadership. There was no running now. I preached my first sermon just two weeks later.

That pastor didn't waste any time. A month after my first sermon, he licensed and ordained me. It was all happening so fast—faster than I could have ever imagined. And yet, just when I thought I had finally found my place, my footing, God threw another curveball my way. A year before his death, that same pastor —the one who had pushed me into ministry—called me into his office. I thought we were just going to talk about Sunday school, but instead, he looked me in the eye and said, *"It's time for you to leave."*

I was stunned. Completely blindsided. How could he ask me to leave the very church where I had found my calling? I cried through the entire service that day, heartbroken and lost. I didn't understand. It felt like a betrayal. I remember telling him, *"I'm waiting on Reynard,"* meaning I was waiting on my husband to get the confirmation from God as well.

And his response, though hard to hear, was a truth that would echo in my spirit long after that day. He said, *"You're waiting on Reynard, but the Lord is waiting on you."*

It felt like a dagger in the moment, but he was right. I had been holding back, waiting on someone else's permission, when God had already given me His. That pastor, in his own way, was releasing me—not out of rejection, but because God had more for me. He commissioned another minister to help me get started in ministry, and I did. I took that step, but believe me, it was a long, slippery road.

There were days I wanted to quit. Days when the weight of it all felt too much to bear. I thought to myself more than once, *"This church thing, this preaching... it's not for me. I'll just do it when I get to heaven."* It seemed easier to push it off to another realm, another time, where I wouldn't have to deal with the struggles of this world. But the reality hit me hard: there's no preaching to be done in heaven. The work we're called to do here, on this earth, has a time limit. In that realm, my work is done. My assignment is graded.

Looking back now, I can see God's hand in everything. What felt like rejection in that pastor's office was actually God protecting me from a future I couldn't see yet. After he passed away, the next pastor who took over that church didn't believe in women preaching. Had I stayed, I would have been trapped, stifled, and silenced again, fighting the same battles I had fought for years. My pastor released me at God's command, to ensure I wouldn't fall back into the pit God had already delivered me from.

Sometimes, God removes us from situations that seem right in our eyes because He sees what's coming. He knows where our purpose will flourish, and where it will wither. And thank God for a pastor who was obedient enough to let me go, even though it must have hurt him too. He was willing to take a loss so that God could get the win.

God is intentional, even concerning you.

He has no plans of ever losing and when you get this, you'll move yourself, misaligned feelings, unchecked emotions, and wicked thoughts out of the way. You'll begin to understand that when it comes to your Creator, there is no questioning His decisions. You either obey or you don't. It's totally up to you. But this my friend, is what makes life challenging and scary. You making your own decisions.

I sometimes feel like my daughter, Raiyawna. I just wish God would have made all the decisions for me and given me a blueprint on everything He willed for me. Then that way, I won't error. I'll stay on track. But the reality is, even then, we would error because the truth is, the Bible is exactly that....our blueprint to better decisions. Yet, we always make the worst choices.

CHAPTER 4
HERE'S THE BLUEPRINT

Have you ever looked at the stars on a clear night and thought about the meticulous design behind them? How each star is placed in a specific position, how they seem scattered yet perfectly aligned, creating constellations that have been used for centuries to guide explorers and dreamers alike? Just like the stars, we too are part of a much bigger design.

Or have you ever thought about the clouds. How they are set and some even resembles shapes of things, people, and places. Have you ever noticed how they seemingly hang in the midst of nowhere having the gravity to stay afloat without dropping or hanging too low. Just like the clouds, God catches keeps us afloat and doesn't allow us to fall too low without giving us warning or transforming our thoughts.

Before we took our first breath, before we even existed in our mother's womb, there was a blueprint for our lives. God, the ultimate architect, didn't just create us haphazardly or by chance. No, He designed each of us with a specific purpose, an intentional plan that we are meant to fulfill. This chapter is about that plan—God's blueprint for your life.

Jeremiah 1:5 – You Were Known Before You Were Born

"Before I formed you in the womb, I knew you; before you were born, I sanctified you; I ordained you a prophet to the nations." – Jeremiah 1:5 (NKJV)

This verse from the book of Jeremiah is one of the clearest affirmations that our lives are not accidents. God tells Jeremiah that before he was even conceived, He already had a plan for him. Think about that for a moment—before *you* were formed, God knew you. Before your first heartbeat, He had already mapped out your journey.

God didn't wait until you were born to decide what you would do. Your existence is not a "let's-see-what-happens" experiment. You are known by God, and He has set you apart for something specific. For Jeremiah, it was to be a prophet to the nations. For you, it might be to lead, to teach, to create, to love, or to serve in ways that only you can.

The blueprint of your life was already in motion before you took your first breath. You were formed with a destiny in mind—a purpose that is woven into your very being.

Ephesians 2:10 – Created for Good Works

"For we are God's handiwork, created in Christ Jesus to do good works, which God prepared in advance for us to do." – Ephesians 2:10 (NIV)

Paul's letter to the Ephesians adds another layer to this understanding of purpose. Here, we are described as God's "handiwork" or "masterpiece" in some translations. Think of an artist who crafts a sculpture with precision and care, who envisions the finished piece long before the first stroke of the chisel. That's how God sees you—His masterpiece, designed to accomplish good works.

Not only are we created by God, but we're created *in Christ Jesus*. This means our purpose isn't just a vague idea or random tasks we stumble upon—it's divinely aligned with the life and mission of Christ. These "good works" aren't just things we decide to do on a whim. They are prepared for us *in advance*. Long before we knew what our talents were, before we even understood the concept of purpose, God had already laid out opportunities for us to walk in.

Your good works—whether they are in ministry, in business, in raising a family, or in creating something beautiful—are part of God's plan. You were made to fulfill them, and no one else can do it the way you can. It's a personal assignment, created with you in mind.

Psalm 139:13-16 – Fearfully and Wonderfully Made

"For you created my inmost being; you knit me together in my mother's womb... My frame was not hidden from you when I was made in the secret place... All the days ordained for me were written in your book before one of them came to be." – Psalm 139:13-16 (NIV)

This passage paints a beautiful picture of God's care and intentionality in creating each of us. David speaks about how God "knit" him together in his mother's womb. Imagine a master craftsman weaving each thread of your being with purpose and precision. You weren't just formed physically; your soul, your gifts, your personality—all of it was intricately woven by the hand of God.

David also writes that "all the days ordained for me were written in your book." This means that God not only created you, but He's also written your story. He knows the highs and the lows, the moments of triumph and the seasons of struggle. Nothing in your life catches God by surprise because every chapter was already planned.

This should give us incredible confidence. Even in the moments where we feel lost or unsure, the blueprint of our lives remains intact. You are *fearfully and wonderfully made* with intentionality that stretches beyond what you can see.

Romans 8:28-30 – Called According to His Purpose

"And we know that in all things God works for the good of those who love him, who have been called according to his purpose." – Romans 8:28 (NIV)

Here's where the blueprint really unfolds. Paul reminds us that we are *called* according to God's purpose. This means that everything in your life, even the things that don't make sense right now, are working together for a greater good. God weaves every experience—whether joyful or painful—into the design He has for your life.

The blueprint is not just about the easy or successful moments. It's about the setbacks, the challenges, the waiting periods. God uses every moment to shape you and prepare you for what He has called you to do. You're being refined, strengthened, and equipped—even when it doesn't feel like it.

When you look back on your life, you'll see how God was aligning everything, even when you were unaware. Every piece of your journey, even the hard parts, are part of your *calling*—a specific assignment that God has set in place for you.

Isaiah 49:1 – Called from the Womb

"Before I was born the Lord called me; from my mother's womb he has spoken my name." – Isaiah 49:1 (NIV)

This verse in Isaiah emphasizes God's personal investment in our lives. He didn't just call you to a task; He *called you by name*. From your mother's womb, He spoke your name with purpose. There's something deeply intimate about this. Before the world knew you, before you were named by your parents, *God* knew you by name.

Your name, your identity, your purpose—they are all interwoven in God's grand design. You weren't chosen randomly; you were specifically called by name. You were on God's mind long before anyone else laid eyes on you.

Understanding the Blueprint

So, what do these scriptures tell us about God's blueprint for our lives?

1. **You were known before you were born (Jeremiah 1:5)** – God's knowledge of you predates your existence. Your purpose was woven into the fabric of your being long before you entered this world.
2. **You were created for good works (Ephesians 2:10)** – There is specific work that only *you* can do. You are God's masterpiece, and your life is designed to fulfill these preordained assignments.
3. **You are fearfully and wonderfully made (Psalm 139:13-16)** – Every detail of your existence is intentional. Your gifts, your quirks, your experiences—all of them serve a purpose in God's plan.
4. **You are called according to His purpose (Romans 8:28)** – Every experience, good or bad, is working together to fulfill God's plan for your life. Nothing is wasted.
5. **You were called by name (Isaiah 49:1)** – Your life is personal to God. He knows you by name, and you were designed to live out a purpose that no one else can fulfill.

The Blueprint is Already Written

As you move forward in life, remember that the blueprint for your existence has already been drawn up by the Master Planner. I know you don't always agree with the plan, but I can assure you that your life will be so much sweeter is you flow with the plan.

Sometimes, it's hard to understand what's good or not good when we are living in a world that always presents right as good, and wrong as right. Yet, you must learn how to discern in order to ensure that you are moving in the right direction and working with the most effective plans. There is work for you.

The question isn't *whether* you have a purpose—it's *how* you will walk in it. It's all around you. It's what makes life more abundant for you. If you never find your purpose, or walk there-in, you will never find the abundant living that God offers as a package of life here on earth.

The closer you get to God, the more the blueprint will be revealed to you. Seek Him, trust the process, and rest in the truth that *you were created with intentionality*. Your life is no accident. You are here because you have been chosen, called, and assigned a unique purpose that only you can fulfill.

Are you ready to step into the blueprint that's been laid out for you?

Or have you made the choice to embrace the alternatives and live just long enough to die?

CHAPTER 5
THE TRAP OF ALTERNATIVES

Yes, that is *heavy*, but it's also the kind of truth we often run from. Society encourages us to choose the safer, more conventional paths, and we sometimes convince ourselves that these choices are just as fulfilling as God's plan. We opt for things that seem more secure—careers, relationships, or material gain—because they're what the world values. They're tangible, easy to measure, and easier to justify to others. But when you ignore the blueprint God has for you, all you're doing is delaying the inevitable.

Listen, when I say, "I had that thing all planned out," I'm not exaggerating. I had my best alternative to serving people. I thought, "Okay, if my role is to save people from the fire, I'll just go ahead and join the fire department." Seemed like a perfect plan, right? Help people, save lives, wear a uniform, do some good.

But now imagine how that could have gone. Imagine how much mess I would have created on that department. Imagine the burden I would've brought into that space—not just for me, but for everyone else around me. If I had pursued that path, I would have been Danyelle the Jonah. And just like Jonah, running from what God told me to do, I would have stirred up storms.

Let's talk about that for a second.

Jonah didn't want to go where God sent him, so he ran in the opposite direction, boarded a ship, and caused a storm that nearly sank everyone with him. The sailors, innocent men trying to do their jobs, were suddenly caught in the middle of Jonah's chaos. And that's what happens when you insert yourself into spaces God hasn't called you to.

We don't like to see ourselves as the problem, but the truth is, when you're not where you're supposed to be, you *become* the problem. You become the portal for turbulence and chaos that wasn't meant to be there in the first place. You start creating ripples of disorder in places that weren't meant for you.

It's no different than stepping into a career you chose just because it felt safe. You might be good at it, but deep down, you know it doesn't align with the purpose God has placed inside of you. You start to feel like something's missing, or worse, you wonder why there's so much resistance.

The same applies to relationships. People jump into relationships or marriages thinking, *"Well, this makes sense,"* or, *"It's better than being alone,"* only to find that this relationship becomes a source of turmoil. It may not even be toxic, but it's distracting you from your true assignment. You pour energy into making it work, but it was never meant to be part of your path. And so the turbulence begins—not just for you, but for the person you're with and for everyone connected to both of you.

This reminds me of broken marriages, actually.

Think about it:

If you've ever been in a relationship or a marriage that wasn't right for you, imagine the ripple effect. Imagine the people around you who were affected—the friends who had to pick up the pieces after a divorce, the children who were caught in the crossfire, the future relationships that carried the baggage of the past. Now, this isn't about guilt, but it's about recognizing the weight of our choices when we move outside of God's plan.

How many lives would have gone a different way if you had stayed in that marriage to the spouse of your youth, *the person you knew deep down was your kingdom partner*? Maybe it would've been a different story if you had followed God's guidance instead of your own understanding. But, here's the reality: some of the drama we experience now, some of the hurt others experience because of us, is simply because we didn't follow God's plan. We stepped out of alignment.

I know that's heavy, but it's the truth.

We carry the bags of drama, confusion, and pain because we didn't stick to the blueprint God laid out for us. And the crazy part is, we often don't realize it until the chaos is fully unleashed. The turbulence doesn't always show up right away. It's subtle at first—maybe just a feeling of unease or restlessness. But as time goes on, it grows, and before you know it, you're in the middle of a full-blown storm.

Distractions are real, and they're dangerous.

The world will encourage you to chase after careers that seem appealing or relationships that make sense on paper. We're taught that having more is better—more success, more money, more social standing, more material gain. But none of that can replace the fulfillment that comes from walking in the purpose God designed specifically for you.

Chasing after *safety* and *appeal* might satisfy you for a moment, but eventually, that empty feeling creeps in because deep down, you know you're not doing what you were created to do. You might be doing good work, but it's not *your* work. You might be in a relationship, but it's not *your* person.

So, let's be real with each other. It's easy to get comfortable in the wrong place, and it's even easier to convince yourself that you're doing the right thing just because it's working on the surface. But deep down, you know when you're not where you're supposed to be.

You feel it. It's like wearing shoes that don't quite fit—sure, you can walk in them, but there's always discomfort, and eventually, it'll start to hurt.

That's what happens when you ignore the blueprint God has for your life and follow what feels *safer* or *more appealing* in the moment. But here's the thing: safety in your own hands is *never* true safety. Real security comes from walking in God's plan because only He knows what's ahead. Only He knows what you were made for, and only He can provide the peace that comes with being in alignment.

When we deviate from that path, when we allow ourselves to get distracted by what the world offers, we not only lose our own footing but, like Jonah, we sometimes bring storms into other people's lives. We carry the weight of unnecessary struggles, simply because we chose what seemed *easier* over what was *ordained*.

So, take a moment. Reflect. Where in your life have you chosen the safer path? What spaces are you occupying that don't belong to you? And how much more peace and purpose could you experience if you trusted the blueprint God already has for your life?

Because trust me, walking in God's purpose may not always feel *safe* by the world's standards, but it will always bring you exactly where you need to be.

Get this...even though the alternative makes a heck of a lot of sense to you, it doesn't. The alternatives can never stand toe-to-toe with the assignment that God has assigned for your life.

When I think of all the time I wasted trying to come up with a substitute for God's plan, I could see how I kept shooting myself in the feet. With every shot I took, healing time was necessary to get back to square root one. How many times have you had to start back at the beginning? Like, who does this to themselves. Keep inflicting wounds that will take time to heal, take years off your life, and add more pain and tears. Yet, we do it all the time when we take the alternatives instead of operating in God's plan.

Then there's the what I want verses what God wants. Of course we always feel like we know what we like better than God, but how can we know when He created us?

Then there's the world. The world will encourage you to chase after careers that seem appealing or relationships that make sense on paper. We're taught that having more is better—more success, more money, more social standing, more material gain. But none of that can replace the fulfillment that comes from walking in the purpose God designed specifically for you.

This is the reason people can gain all of these things and still be the most miserable persons on earth. I think I learned this too the hard way.

Oh, I wanted a big house on a lot of land. I chased it until I got it and that house saw more problems than I will care to share. Children went ham. Husband started going left, and I got so caught up in getting more until the devil was killing, stealing, and destroying everything we'd built and we didn't even know, recognize, or realize it. We were chasing everything except God, and the devil was working his assignment to perfection and getting the job done.

Chasing after *safety* and *appeal* might satisfy you for a moment, but eventually, that empty feeling creeps in because deep down, you know you're not doing what you were created to do. You might be doing good work, but it's not *your* work. You might be in a relationship, but it's not *your* person. And anytime you chase after stuff, things, and people that don't belong to you, you take the hits.

Let me tell you…one does not always bounce back from these hits the way he or she would like. Some hits kill you. I think I'll repeat that for the one who has gotten comfortable taking hits… SOME HITS KILL YOU.

You don't always bounce back the way you once did, the way you used too, or the way you expect to. Some of these things will hurt you so bad to your core until they drive you insane. I know some folks who have taken some hits that have ran them crazy. They've lost so much and so big, until there is no way to shake back in their mind or eyes.

And it's a dangerous place when we accept defeat to the point that we don't believe that even God can deliver us from.

So, let's talk about what happens when you run from your assignment—because sometimes, we think we know better. We think our plan is safer, easier, or more convenient. But there's a danger in resisting the calling on your life, and Jonah is the perfect example of this.

CHAPTER 6

THE STORY OF JONAH RUNNING

In Jonah 1:1-3, the Bible tells us:
"The word of the Lord came to Jonah son of Amittai: 'Go to the great city of Nineveh and preach against it, because its wickedness has come up before me.' But Jonah ran away from the Lord and headed for Tarshish. He went down to Joppa, where he found a ship bound for that port. After paying the fare, he went aboard and sailed for Tarshish to flee from the Lord."

God gave Jonah a clear and direct assignment—go to Nineveh and preach against its wickedness. But Jonah wanted no part of it. Maybe the task seemed too hard, too dangerous, or simply not something he wanted to do. So, instead of obeying God's instructions, Jonah *ran*.

Now, when we hear this story, it's easy to think, *How could Jonah be so foolish?* But here's the thing: we do this all the time. God places a calling on our lives, but because we're afraid, uncertain, or uncomfortable, we run in the opposite direction. Like Jonah, we convince ourselves that we can flee from God's assignment.

Jonah didn't just ignore his calling—he actively fled from it. He boarded a ship bound for Tarshish, which was literally in the opposite direction of Nineveh. And what happened? Jonah's disobedience didn't just affect him; it had a ripple effect on everyone around him.

The Consequences of Running from God's Will

While Jonah was on that ship, trying to escape God's call, a great storm came upon the sea. The Bible says it was so violent that the ship threatened to break apart (Jonah 1:4). The sailors on board were terrified, crying out to their gods and throwing cargo overboard to lighten the ship. They had no idea that Jonah was the cause of their turmoil.

That's what happens when we try to run from God's plan—we bring storms into places that were never meant to experience them. People around us suffer because we're not where we're supposed to be. Just like Jonah, when we resist God's calling, it doesn't only disrupt our own lives—it disrupts the lives of others too.

The sailors finally confronted Jonah and asked him who he was and why this disaster had come upon them. Jonah admitted, *"I am a Hebrew and I worship the Lord, the God of heaven, who made the sea and the dry land"* (Jonah 1:9). He knew exactly why the storm had come. He knew it was because he was running from God's assignment. He told the sailors, *"Pick me up and throw me into the sea… and it will become calm. I know that it is my fault that this great storm has come upon you"* (Jonah 1:12).

The sailors, reluctant but desperate, threw Jonah overboard—and as soon as they did, the storm stopped. Jonah's disobedience had caused a storm, and it wasn't until he was removed from the situation that peace returned.

Here's the lesson: Running from your assignment doesn't just bring chaos into your own life—it often brings chaos into the lives of those around you. When you try to operate in a space that isn't meant for you, you end up bringing disorder and turbulence where there should be peace. You may not see yourself as the cause of the problem, but like Jonah, your resistance to God's plan creates storms. And sometimes, those storms impact innocent people—family, friends, coworkers—who are caught up in the consequences of your disobedience.

But here's the beauty of God's plan: even when we run, He doesn't abandon us. Even when we resist, God's purpose for our lives remains intact. After Jonah was thrown overboard, the Bible tells us that God provided a great fish to swallow him, and Jonah was in the belly of the fish for three days and three nights (Jonah 1:17). In that dark, confined space, Jonah had time to reflect on his disobedience, and eventually, he repented. He prayed to the Lord from inside the fish, acknowledging God's mercy and sovereignty.

Jonah wasn't released until he submitted to God's will. And when he finally obeyed, God gave him another chance to fulfill his assignment. He was spit out on dry land, and the word of the Lord came to him a second time, saying, *"Go to the great city of Nineveh and proclaim to it the message I give you"* (Jonah 3:1-2). This time, Jonah obeyed.

Jonah's story teaches us that no matter how far we run, we can't escape the call God has placed on our lives. The blueprint He has for us is non-negotiable. We can try to take detours or delay it, but eventually, we have to come face-to-face with the truth: *There's no peace, no fulfillment, no blessing outside of God's will.*

How often do we, like Jonah, choose to run from our God-given assignments? Maybe God is calling you to a career or a ministry that feels too intimidating. Maybe there's a relationship He's asking you to step away from, or one He's pushing you toward, but fear and doubt are holding you back. Or maybe, like Jonah, you're just tired of the demands of your calling and you want to take the easy way out.

When you step outside of God's will, it might seem like the easier path at first. Maybe there's a sense of relief in doing something that feels more "manageable." But just as Jonah learned, that relief is temporary. It won't be long before the storms start to rise, and you'll realize that the very thing you were trying to escape was meant for your good.

You see, when God gives you an assignment, it's not to make your life harder—it's to bring you into alignment with His purpose for your life. When you run from that, you end up creating turbulence, not only for yourself but for those around you.

Think of the people you've affected when you've strayed from your calling. The careers that didn't work out, the relationships that fell apart, the projects that stalled—these were all consequences of stepping out of alignment with God's plan.

But the good news is this: *God is merciful.* Just like Jonah, you can always turn back. God will provide a way back into His will when you submit to His calling. The storms will calm, and the path forward will be made clear. But it starts with obedience. It starts with stepping into the assignment He's already placed on your life.

So, I ask you today—where are you running? And more importantly, when will you stop?

CHAPTER 7
DISTRACTIONS THAT PULL

One of the biggest challenges in walking out your God-given purpose isn't necessarily knowing what that purpose is. For many, the real struggle comes when distractions, temptations, and seemingly "good" opportunities start to pull us away from the path we were created to follow. It doesn't always happen all at once. Sometimes the pull is subtle, disguised as a harmless detour or even as a blessings. Listen, all blessings don't come from heaven and they all aren't orchestrated by God. These distractions, that comes in forms of blessings, can slowly nudge you further and further from where God is calling you to be.

We're going to talk about how to recognize when you're being pulled away from your purpose and, more importantly, how to stay grounded, avoid temptation, and stay laser-focused on the path God has for you. Because believe me, there will come a time when distraction will creep like a mice. Have you ever had a rat or mice? I know. Disgusting; but I live in the country, and every time they cut the field behind my house, if I'm not ready, then I have to kill mice.

Now, what's crazy to me is how they never come out in the daytime. I guess field mice or smarter. They start to roam at night, when the house is totally quiet, and when they can get in and go out undetected. That's just how distractions designed to pull you off track works. They come out when you least expect them. During times when you aren't looking for them. And most of the time, they are as quiet as a church mice.

You don't know they've been there until they start to leave the residue of their visit behind. But get this…crap that pull you away from your purpose don't always stink. Like those rat turds. Sometimes, you don't even notice it's a turd until you take a closer look.

Baby, you better learn how to use the spirit of discernment so you can get a closer look into the things that are trying to distract you from your purpose. The first step in staying on track is being able to recognize when you're being pulled away from your purpose. It's not always obvious—distractions can be sneaky. They often come disguised as good opportunities, as relationships that feel fulfilling in the moment, or as career choices that seem practical. But deep down, if you're paying attention, you'll notice that these distractions pull you further away from what God has placed on your heart.

Like the mice leaves turds, so does a drift away from your purpose. Let's take a look at them.

1. You Feel Restless or Unfulfilled

One of the clearest signs that you're not aligned with your purpose is a sense of restlessness or un-fulfillment. No matter how much I think things are going great, there's always this bad energy that keeps me looking around like I'm waiting on something bad to happen. Even when things seem to be going good, inside, there's a gnawing feeling or turmoil that something just isn't quite right. You might feel unsettled at the job-like there's a hidden enemy. In your relationships-like a sidepiece could pop up at any moment. Or your daily routine-like if I go in one more store I might catch covid. No matter how much you try to push that feeling down, it keeps resurfacing, whispering that something is missing.

Restlessness is often one of the ways God nudges us back to our true purpose. When you're out of alignment with His plan, no amount of success, money, or external validation will fill that void. It's like a car with new tires. Doesn't matter that you put the most expensive tires on the car. If you don't get it aligned, it will ride just as bumpy as those old tires did. That's what it feels like to ride restless or unfulfilled.

2. You're Chasing Short-Term Wins Over Long-Term Purpose

You may be straying from your actual purpose if you find yourself looking for fast solutions, simple rewards, or rapid fulfillment all the time. This is exactly why I stay away from stuff that says you can make money quick. Anything quick means, I'm settling. I don't want to work for what I'm asking God for. Sometimes, we lose sight of the broader vision God intends for our life because we are so preoccupied with pursuing the things that will bring us instant satisfaction, whether it be money, attention, or approval.

Come-ups that come quickly might be alluring, especially if they provide a momentary sensation of fulfillment. However, they frequently divert our attention from the more in-depth, purposeful task that has been given to us. They cause us to get caught up in happy moments instead of complete joy. And trust me there's a huge different in joy and happiness. These small victories are ephemeral, chasing after what seems wonderful in the moment might leave you feeling empty and drained; especially dealing with relationships. They can leave you feeling used and abused. When you're living out your purpose, the reward might not come immediately, but it's lasting and fulfilling in ways that short-term success never could be.

3. You're Constantly Facing Unnecessary Obstacles

Believe me, every journey has its challenges, but if you're constantly running into walls, facing resistance, or struggling to make progress, it could be a sign that you're on the wrong path. I say if I run into obstacles, "This isn't what God wants for me." Because every time I have jumped over an obstacle. Destruction catches up to me. Sometimes, we think that if we work harder or push through, everything will eventually fall into place. But here's the thing—when you're walking in God's purpose for your life, there's a grace that comes with it.

That's not to say that everything will be easy, but there's a difference between the natural challenges of growth and the unnecessary roadblocks that come from stepping outside of God's plan. Listen…God is always speaking to us when we in His will. Sometimes, His word is simply "NO," from the lips of someone else.

I got some stories for you, but every time something, someone, some place, isn't for me…God always puts a reason from me to turn away from that place. Every time I turn and go back, I take a hit. If everything feels like an uphill battle, it's worth asking if you're pursuing the wrong thing, trying to make something work that was never meant for you.

4. You're Surrounded by Distractions

One of the enemy's greatest tools is distraction. And these distractions often come in forms that seem harmless—or even beneficial. A new relationship, a career opportunity, or a side hustle that seems promising—can all be planted distractions that come to pull you off course. These things pull your focus away from your God-given mission, they're not just distractions—they're detours.

Distractions can also come in the form of busyness. Oh my God Marthas…sit down somewhere. I get nervous around people who do too much. It's the little things God shows us that can take you from sitting at His feet and learning of Him. Do I have any Mary's in the house? You see the distractions Martha busy with, but you ain't got time for that. Why? You are trying to get where God has promised. Busy work can make you miss good opportunities to advance. Don't be so overwhelmed by tasks, responsibilities, or projects that you no longer have the time or energy to pursue the things that really matter. Pay attention to what's consuming your time and ask yourself if these activities are helping or hindering your walk in God's purpose.

5. You're Seeking Validation from Others Instead of God

When you find yourself constantly looking for approval or validation from people—whether that's friends, family, or even colleagues—you're on shaky ground. Your purpose comes from God, not from people. If you can honestly say that you are more focused on what others think about you—than on what God has called you to do—you'll find yourself compromising your values, your vision, and your direction.

Everything we watch on the news concerning people doing nasty stuff to come up. Or as I call it…something strange for some change. These are they who wanted man to elevate them instead of God. It's easy to get caught up in seeking praise or recognition, but people's opinions are fickle. They change. God's plan for you, does not. When you're aligned with His will, the only approval you need is His.

My people look at me crazy when they finally get close enough to me to know I could care less about people. I love them. I'm called to get them saved. But I'm wise enough to know they won't always like what I say or how I move. Their validation means nothing. And the strangest thing I've learned…if people like you, then God ain't using you. Don't get caught in the trap of getting the pat on the back.

The same people who pat you today can spit on you tomorrow. Don't go down having pleased man and not God.

How to Stay Focused on Your Purpose

Now that we've looked at how to recognize when you're being pulled away from your purpose, let's dive into some practical tips for staying on course. God's path for you might not always be easy, but it's always worth it. It might not always require the same things that mine did, but I can almost guarantee you that something here will hit you in the gut. Here's how to stay focused and avoid temptation:

1. Stay Rooted in Prayer and God's Word

The best way to stay aligned with your purpose is to stay connected to the One who created it. Prayer is your lifeline, weapon, speed bumped, petition, guard rails, must I keep going? It's your direct connection to God, and one of the keys to how you receive guidance, peace, directives, instructions, stoplights, hazard signs, and clarity. Again, must I go on?

When you start to have regular time in prayer, it not only strengthens your relationship with God but also keeps you grounded when distractions come your way. It builds a fence all around you. Fred Hammond sings a song, "Jesus Be A Fence." I love it because I found out that the way to get Him to be that fence is to pray.

No here is my number one way to stay focused: Spending time in God's Word. This is just as crucial as prayer. The Bible is full of wisdom and direction, and it's where God will often reveal truths about your purpose. When you immerse yourself in scripture, you begin to see things more clearly. The Word of God helps you to be better equipped to recognize when something is pulling you off course.

Just as sure as my name is Danyelle, as soon as I'm leaning in the wrong direction, whether it my morning manna, The Daily Bread, or even my son, D.J. Gatlin, somehow, the Word always comes and convicts me and puts me back on the right road.

2. Learn to Say "No" to Good Things

Not every opportunity that comes your way is from God. Sometimes, you have to say "no" to good things so you can say "yes" to the *right* things. This can be hard, especially when an opportunity seems promising or when you're tempted to please others.

This summer everyone was calling me to honor me. As much as I wanted to say, 'yes,' my heart wouldn't let me. The question I said to myself is: have you done anything to be rewarded. Are you seeking man's reward's or God's? When I couldn't answer as I knew I needed, I declined. Just because something looks good or people think you are worth celebrating, doesn't mean it's God's plan for you.

Discernment is key.

I sought the Lord for an answer and amidst my daughter saying, "Mommy you're worthy of honor." And her dad saying, "Dan, don't miss your opportunities." I still felt a 'no to those things' in my heart. Take every opportunity, every relationship, and every decision to God in prayer. Ask for His guidance before you commit. If you feel uneasy, if you sense a lack of peace, or if it seems to pull you away from your ultimate mission, it's okay to walk away.

3. Surround Yourself with Purpose-Driven People

Who you surround yourself with matters. If you're spending time with people who don't share your values or your vision, it's easy to get pulled off track. Surround yourself with purpose-driven people—those who encourage you, challenge you, and hold you accountable to your calling.

You need people in your life who will remind you of your God-given purpose, especially in moments of doubt. Iron sharpens iron, and when you're in community with others who are focused on their own purpose, you'll find it easier to stay focused on yours.

4. Guard Your Heart and Mind

The Bible tells us to *"guard your heart above all else, for it determines the course of your life"* (Proverbs 4:23, NLT). Your heart and mind are the gateways to your purpose. What you allow into your heart and mind—whether through relationships, television, music, sexual entertainment, or even the conversations you have—can impact your focus. And we all know, the devil is so cunning. He will take the smallest of events and corrupt them on a large scale if it means he breaks your focus.

Be mindful of what you consume. Whether it's social media, TV shows, or conversations with friends, ask yourself if these things are helping or hindering your walk with God. By all means, laughter is good for your soul, but be careful of the videos you watch. At some point, people were sending me videos and I was falling the rabbit holes of one after the other after the other.

Before long, I'd spent thirty minutes of my life, laughing at foolishness. Who was the fool? The enemy loves to use subtle distractions to pull you off course, so be diligent about what you allow into your heart and mind.

5. Keep the End Goal in Mind

It's easy to get distracted when you lose sight of the bigger picture. When you keep your focus on the ultimate goal—fulfilling the purpose God has for your life—everything will start to fall into place. Remind yourself of the calling upon your life and who placed it there. Write it down. Pray over it. Meditate on the promises God has given you. Rehearse the prophecies spoken over your life. Pray for your expected end. All of this matters when you are chasing after what God has for you.

When you keep the end goal in mind, the temporary temptations and distractions of this world will seem far less appealing. You'll be able to push through difficult seasons because you know the work you're doing is kingdom work—it has eternal value.

Closing Thoughts

Recognizing when you're being pulled away from your purpose is half the battle. The world, what it has to offer, and the devil who controls it will constantly try to distract you, tempt you, and pull you away from the path God has set for you. But when you're rooted in prayer, guided by God's Word, and surrounded by people who encourage your growth, you'll have the clarity and strength to stay focused.

Your purpose isn't just a random assignment—it's a divine blueprint. The closer you stay to God, the clearer that blueprint will become. I promise if you stay on your seeking game, the easier it will be to navigate the distractions and temptations that come your way.

So, the next time you feel that pull, take a step back. Reflect. Pray. And ask yourself: *Is this taking me closer to the purpose God has for my life?*

And if the answer is no, turn from that thing.

An Affirmation For Your Life

I thank You for my purpose.

Your promise is rich in me, and for me it is yes and amen. No fear, doubts, or insecurities will block or hinder my purpose.

I will not turn away from my goal or be distracted.

I will accomplish all that You have set before me to accomplish. Everything I have need of is already mine.

Every door is opened, every financial matter is solved. Every victory is won. And every assignment is complete.

No things, people, places, money, heights, or depths will separate me from my goals, gifts, and the purpose You have placed upon my life.

I am blessed. I am highly favored. I am the seed of Abraham. And, I have all things in me to perfect, and finish my assignment.

If you desire...write our your own affirmations.

CHAPTER 8

OVERCOMING FEAR & DOUBT

If there's two things that can paralyze even the strongest believer: fear and doubt. These two emotions have a way of creeping into your heart. Their goal is to slowly weaken your confidence in what God has said, and what He has called you to do. They can make you question your ability to do, your worth and desire to do, and even God's plan for your life. Here is the one thing we all must remember: no matter how much fear and doubt try to overwhelm you, there is hope.

You are strong enough to overcome fear and doubt—not by ignoring them, but by facing them head-on with the truth of God's Word. The Father has already equipped you, even when you don't feel ready, and your prayer life is how you push past the doubts that threaten to derail your purpose.

Listen, if God said it, that settles it. All you have to do is know enough of God's Word to call Him to that. I tell my church family almost every Sunday this:

"So will My word be which goes out of My mouth; It will not

return to Me empty, Without accomplishing what I desire, And without succeeding *in the purpose* for which I sent it" (Isaiah 55:11 NASB).

You have to believe what He has already spoken. You also have to remember that fear and doubt are like two sides of the same coin. Or, they are both from the devil talking out of both sides of his mouth. Fear tells you that you're not enough, that the obstacles are too great, that you will fail. Doubt whispers that God isn't with you, that His promises won't come through, and that you've somehow misunderstood His calling for your life.

These emotions aren't new. Their tactics aren't new. The devil has been using these two from the days he spoke to Eve in the garden. These are the very two accomplishes he used to cause Eve to persuade her husband into disobeying God. They've also been around since the beginning of time, and they've tried to stop some of the greatest biblical heroes from fulfilling their purposes. Moses doubted his ability to lead Israel out of Egypt. Gideon was afraid to rise up as a leader. Even the Apostle Peter, one of Jesus's closest disciples, was filled with fear and doubt when he stepped out onto the water.

But in each of these stories, we also see the key to overcoming these powerful emotions: faith. Faith that God's strength is greater than our weakness, that His power is made perfect in our weakness, and that He *will* fulfill His promises. Everything He has said in His Word is truth.

But get this…

The feeling fear or doubt doesn't disqualify you from walking in your purpose. In fact, it's often a sign that you're on the verge of something significant. The enemy uses fear and doubt as tools to keep you stuck because he knows what God is about to do through you.

See, anyone stuck doesn't have the ability to move. But anyone moving, has the power to go places stuck folks only dream about. Baby, don't allow the enemy to keep you stuck. If they can make you stuck, then they can control you.

But here's the truth: **fear and doubt don't have to control you**. They may come, but they don't have to stay. You can move forward in faith, even when you're afraid or uncertain. Let's look at ways to move beyond our fears.

1. Acknowledge the Fear, but Don't Let It Stop You

One of the greatest misconceptions is that you have to wait until fear is gone before you move forward. But that's not true. The key to overcoming fear isn't waiting for it to disappear—it's moving forward *in spite* of it.

Look at the story of Gideon. When God called him to lead Israel against the Midianites, Gideon was hiding in a winepress. Dude was terrified of the enemy. And just like us, he had the same strikes in cue: he didn't feel qualified, strong, or brave. Nevertheless, God called him anyway, and then for faith's sake, God addresses him as a "mighty warrior" (Judges 6:12). Gideon didn't see himself that way, but just like him, we have to see ourselves as God sees us to overcome fear.

Did the fear vanish immediately? No. But Gideon moved forward, step by step, in obedience. And in doing so, he saw God's power work through him in ways he never imagined.

Listen, you don't have to wait for fear to leave you before you answer God's call. Take the first step, even if your knees are shaking, your stomach is queasy, and your head is dizzy. God's strength will meet you in your obedience.

2. Replace Doubt with Truth

Doubt comes when we believe lies—lies about who we are, about God's power, and about our circumstances. The devil is the father of lies and if he can get you to believe the lies...he can block the vision and plans for your life. The only way to defeat doubt is to replace it with truth. And that truth is found in God's Word.

Every time doubt whispers that you're not enough, remember what God says about you. You are His masterpiece, created for good works (Ephesians 2:10). You are chosen, called, and equipped (1 Peter 2:9). You are fearfully and wonderfully made (Psalm 139:14). God's Word is filled with promises about your identity and your purpose.

Whenever doubt tries to creep in, go to the Word. Speak God's promises out loud. Use His Word to remind yourself of the truth, and let that truth drive out the lies.

When Jesus was tempted in the wilderness, He didn't fight the enemy with His feelings—He fought with the Word of God. He didn't cuss or tell the enemy off. Each time Satan tried to plant doubt in His mind, Jesus responded with Scripture. If Jesus, the Son of God, used the Word to fight off doubt, how much more do we need to do the same?

Like for real! How much more are you going to have to have some WORD BULLETS in order to shoot the devil in his lips? You need them friends and that's no lie.

3. Focus on God's Ability, Not Yours

One of the reasons fear and doubt are so effective is because they get us to focus on our own limitations, circumstances, and situations. We look at the size of the task ahead, the obstacles in our way, what we don't have, who we don't know, and our other weaknesses, and it becomes easy to doubt if we can do what God has called us to do. But here's the thing: God isn't asking you to rely on *our* strength. He's asking you to rely on *His*.

Moses doubted his ability to speak, but God reminded him that He is the one who gave Moses his mouth (Exodus 4:11-12). God didn't expect Moses to lead in his own strength—He simply needed Moses to trust that His strength was enough.

When you're faced with fear and doubt, shift the focus from your inadequacies and focus on God's sufficiency. The Bible says, *"Not by might nor by power, but by my Spirit,' says the Lord Almighty"* (Zechariah 4:6). It's not about what you can or can't do; it's always about what God can and will do through you.

Remember: God never calls you to something that He hasn't already equipped you to do. The work might be beyond your ability, but it's not beyond His. The wisdom to do the work is one prayer away. The plans to accomplish the task is just one prayer and faith act away.

Trust God all the way.

4. Take It One Step at a Time

One of the reasons fear and doubt can be so paralyzing is that we try to see the whole journey at once; we try to piece together the entire puzzle in one setting. We want to know how everything will work out before we take the first step. But that's not how faith works.

God often calls us to take steps of obedience without showing us the entire picture. Look at Abraham—God called him to leave his home and go to a land that He would show him *later* (Genesis 12:1). Abraham didn't have the full picture, but he trusted God and took the first step.

When I decided to write books. I didn't know what to do except how to write or type. That's it. Didn't even know what I was going to write about. Now eighty-eight books later, all I can tell you is that if you take one step, God will take eighty-seven more.

When fear and doubt try to overwhelm you, break it down step by step. First write the book. Second, find the editor. Third, find a publisher. Forth, find a cover maker. See...if you do it step by step, it's less overwhelming. What's the next step God is asking you to take? Focus on that, and trust that when it's time for the next step, God will guide you.

Faith isn't about having all the answers. It's not about seeing the complete picture. It's about trusting the One who does. Take it one step at a time, and trust that God will lead you exactly where you need to go.

5. Remember God's Faithfulness

When fear and doubt try to take hold, it's easy to forget how far God has already brought you. One of the most powerful ways to overcome fear and doubt is to remember God's faithfulness in the past. Look back over your life at all the times when God provided, when He opened doors, when He made a way where there seemed to be no way, and when He brought you out.

In Joshua 4, after the Israelites crossed the Jordan River, God instructed them to set up memorial stones to remind them of how He had delivered them. These stones were meant to be a visual reminder of God's faithfulness, so that when doubt arose, they could look back and remember that the same God who parted the waters was still with them.

Dear friends, you've got to learn how to set some stones out. I got a stone over each one of my children and my husband, on how God will deliver you from death. There's a stone named Alma (my momma) of how He will heal you from cancer. There's a stone named Joe-my dad—on how you can live years after a bone cancer diagnosis. Baby! I've got some stones that don't even belong to me.

Some of my stones is set because I watched God bring you out. I watched Him turn your situation around and I decided, if He could do it for you, He can do it for me. Don't mess around and allow your stones to give me strength and do nothing for you. You better act like you know...when fear tries to rise up, remind yourself of God's faithfulness. If He did it before, He can do it again.

6. Surround Yourself with Encouragers

The people you surround yourself with have a huge impact on how you handle fear and doubt. If you're constantly around people who doubt your abilities or question your calling, it will be hard to move in faith. But if you surround yourself with people who encourage you, who remind you of God's promises, and who push you to trust God, you'll find it much easier to overcome fear and doubt.

Look at the story of David and Goliath. Before David went out to face the giant, his own brothers and even King Saul doubted him. But David's faith was stronger than their doubts. David remembered how God had delivered him from lions and bears in the past (1 Samuel 17:34-37).

Sometimes you have to quiet the voices of doubt around you and remind yourself of what God has done and said. Seek out people who will speak life into you. Find friends who will remind you of your calling and who will stand with you in prayer when fear tries to creep in.

I hate being around people. When I'm not preaching…I'm weird, guarded, shy, all of that. But I have a friend named Stormy Gage-Watts. This girl can pull me outside even when I'm hiding. I love the fact that she's encouraged enough by my gift to want me to be known. This is what you need. People who see you as God does.

Last Thoughts:

Fear and doubt are natural, but they don't have to control your life or your actions. Overcoming them is a process of faith—trusting that God's promises are greater than your fears, that His strength is greater than your weakness. His purpose for you will be fulfilled if you continue to walk in obedience. So the next time fear and doubt come knocking at your door, don't let them in. Instead, stand on God's Word, remember His faithfulness and His promises. Fight to take steps forward, even when you don't feel ready.

Your purpose is too important to let fear and doubt steal it from you. And the God who called you is more than able to bring you through every storm and test.

CHAPTER 9

THE STORY OF MOSES: RELUCTANCE

There's something deeply human about feeling unqualified. When God calls us to something beyond what we think we can handle, it's natural to hesitate, to question, and to even say, "Not me, Lord." Few stories in the Bible capture this kind of reluctance better than the story of Moses. God called Moses to a monumental task—one that would free an entire nation from oppression—but Moses's immediate response wasn't one of bold faith.

It was fear, doubt, and a long list of reasons why he wasn't the right man for the job. His story shows us that even the greatest leaders in biblical history sometimes doubted their abilities and feared stepping into the roles God had prepared for them. Sometimes, I really wonder how Dr. Martin Luther King Jr. felt. To see him carry such a burden is a stark reminder of what Jesus saw and felt.

It's also a story of how God reassures, equips, and stands by those He calls. No matter how unqualified they feel, when God says

'It's you,' cousin, friend, kinfolks, old folks, young'uns, whoever... IT IS YOU!

Let's dive into Moses's story in *Exodus 3 and 4*, examining his hesitation, his excuses, and the way God patiently reassured him that the calling was bigger than Moses's weaknesses. If you've ever doubted your own abilities or felt unworthy of God's call, Moses's journey offers hope and shows us how God works through our reluctance.

The Calling of Moses (Exodus 3:1-10)

Moses's story begins long before the burning bush, but it's in *Exodus 3* where we see the moment that would change the course of his life. At this point, Moses was living a quiet, isolated life in Midian. He has fled Egypt after killing an Egyptian and now worked as a shepherd for his father-in-law, Jethro. It seemed like Moses's story might end here—hidden, forgotten, far away from the grandeur of Egypt and his people's suffering.

But God had other plans.

While Moses is tending to the flock, he sees a burning bush that isn't being consumed by the flames. Out of curiosity, he approaches the bush, and it is there that God calls to him, saying, *"Moses, Moses!"* And Moses responds with a simple, *"Here I am"* (Exodus 3:4).

Now, what gets me is that Moses didn't say, "Who are you?" My first response had I been called out of the blue. But the fact that he says, *"Here I am,"* leads me to believe that when God calls us, we already know He sees us, and we already know we might as well answer.

God tells Moses that He has seen the oppression of His people in Egypt, and that He is going to deliver them from their slavery. And then came the moment that Moses likely never saw coming:

"So now, go. I am sending you to Pharaoh to bring my people the Israelites out of Egypt" (Exodus 3:10).

Moses, the runaway, the exile, the shepherd—God was sending him back to Egypt, the place of his greatest failure, to face Pharaoh and lead an entire nation to freedom. Moses probably feels like my greatest character of all time—Arnold from Different Strokes. Instead of 'What you talking about Willis?' Moses probably wanted to say, 'What You tripping off of God?'

So here starts Moses's reluctance and excuses (Exodus 3:11-4:13)

Moses didn't respond to this call with excitement or confidence. Instead, he responded with hesitation and doubt. His reluctance poured out in a series of excuses, each one revealing his deep fear and sense of inadequacy. Let's break down his responses:

1. "Who am I?" (Exodus 3:11)

Moses's first response was one of self-doubt. He asked, *"Who am I that I should go to Pharaoh and bring the Israelites out of Egypt?"* Moses couldn't comprehend how God could use someone like him—a man with a troubled past, a fugitive, someone who had spent the last 40 years as a shepherd in the desert, and someone who knew all too well what went down in Pharaoh's house.

But God didn't answer Moses by affirming his abilities. Instead, God reassured him with His presence: *"I will be with you"* (Exodus 3:12). God's message to Moses is clear—this wasn't about Moses's capabilities or worthiness. It was about God's power working through him. When God calls us, it's not about who we are; it's about *who He is and what He can do when He works through us.*

Our past, limitations, weaknesses, lack of, misguided energy, barely educated, skin color, body weight, or our sins—none of it disqualifies us when God is the one empowering us.

2. "What if they don't believe me?" (Exodus 4:1)

Moses's second excuse has the root of fear of rejection. He said, *"What if they do not believe me or listen to me and say, 'The Lord did not appear to you'?"* This fear is something many of us can relate to—what if others don't believe in our calling? What if they doubt that God is really with us?

God didn't leave Moses hanging. He equipped him with tangible signs to prove His power. God told Moses to throw his staff on the ground, and it turned into a snake. When Moses picked it up, it became a staff again. God then gave Moses two more signs: turning his hand leprous and then healing it, and turning water from the Nile into blood (Exodus 4:2-9). These signs were meant to reassure Moses that God's power would be visible, and the people would believe because of what they saw.

Sometimes, when we step out in faith, we worry about whether others will recognize God's hand on our lives. But just like with Moses, God will give all the confirmation you need. He will equip you with the tools necessary to fulfill your calling. People will see the evidence of God working through you, even if they doubt at first.

Here's another thing. God will make you ask the people who doubt you, if they believe you. Then when they lie, God will show them the evidence of Him in you, and cause them to reap the lie upon their heads that they spoke in their disbelief.

3. "I'm not good enough" (Exodus 4:10)

Moses continued to resist, offering yet another excuse: "Pardon your servant, Lord. I have never been eloquent, neither in the past nor since you have spoken to your servant. I am slow of speech and tongue" (Exodus 4:10).

Moses didn't think he was a good speaker, and he felt that his inadequacy in this area made him unfit for the task. Sort of reminds me of Jeremiah who didn't think he could be a prophet because of his age. This is something we all experience at some point—feeling like we're not skilled enough, smart enough, or talented enough to do what God has called us to do. We highlight our flaws and limitations, thinking they disqualify us from God's purpose. But when God calls us, let me write this in bold and CAPS so you can get it even if your eyes are dim...**GOD EQUIPS THOSE HE CALLS.**

But God's response to Moses was both powerful and convicting: "Who gave human beings their mouths? Who makes them deaf or mute? Who gives them sight or makes them blind? Is it not I, the Lord? Now go; I will help you speak and will teach you what to say" (Exodus 4:11-12).

God didn't need Moses to be an eloquent speaker—He simply needed Moses to be willing. And that's what God asks of us. He doesn't need us to be perfect or highly skilled in every area; He just needs us to be available and obedient. He will supply what we lack.

4. "Please send someone else" (Exodus 4:13)

Despite all the reassurances, Moses still pleaded with God to send someone else. *"Pardon your servant, Lord. Please send someone else"* (Exodus 4:13). This final plea reveals how deep Moses's fear and reluctance was. Even after all the signs and assurances, he still didn't believe he was the right person for the job.

God's response shows both His patience and His resolve. While God did become angry with Moses, He still provided a solution. God told Moses that his brother Aaron could speak on his behalf, but Moses would still lead (Exodus 4:14-16).

God didn't let Moses off the hook. The calling remained, but He gave Moses the support he needed. Sometimes, even when we're fearful, God will place people in our lives to help us along the way, but He doesn't abandon the assignment. He remains steadfast in His call for us.

For me that was a lady named Linda Baldwin. God didn't let me out of the assignment, he placed this woman in my life to show me what real faith in God looks like. How, if you trust God, God will do exactly what He has said concerning you. I thank God for this woman and her life of faith, because every time I'm up against something that seems too much or too big, she becomes my stone.

For every insecurity Moses had, God provided a solution:

- "Who am I?" → "I will be with you."
- "What if they don't believe me?" → "Here are signs to prove My power."
- "I'm not a good speaker." → "I will help you speak."
- "Please send someone else." → "I'll send Aaron to help you."

God didn't just call Moses to an impossible task and leave him to figure it out. He equipped him with what he needed and reassured him every step of the way. Moses's story shows us that God doesn't require us to be perfect, fearless, or fully confident. He requires us to be *willing*.

If you get nothing else from this book, I need you to get this: GOD QUALIFIES THE CALLED.

He doesn't choose us based upon our qualification, skill sets, confidence levels, or abilities that go hand in hand with the job description. He chooses us based upon His purpose and reasoning for creating us.

Let's recap so you can learn some pivotal keys from Moses's life.

1. God Sees Beyond Your Limitations

Moses saw himself as unworthy, unqualified, and inadequate. But God saw beyond his faults and fears. When God looks at you,

He doesn't just see your weaknesses—He sees your potential, your calling, your assignment, and His power working through you.

As the apostle Paul writes in 2 Corinthians 12:9, *"My grace is sufficient for you, for my power is made perfect in weakness."* Your weaknesses don't disqualify you—they actually position you to rely on God's strength.

2. Your Fear Doesn't Dismiss Your Calling

Moses was afraid, and his fear didn't disappear right away. Yet, God didn't change His mind about calling Moses to lead the Israelites out of Egypt. Your fear doesn't scare God; nor does the fear of those who are trying to block you. Can it be that men are fearful that if women preach, we will take over? I'm not certain. But when God calls a real woman of God, she desires to help the brethren, not harm them. Fear is a normal part of walking in faith, but it doesn't have the final say.

3. God Provides Everything You Need

When God calls you to something, He equips those He calls. He supplies you with the tools, words, wisdom, and the strength to carry out His assignment. Just as God provided Moses with signs, a staff, and the help of Aaron, He will provide for you. It might not always be in the way you expect, but God will always ensure you have what you need to fulfill His purpose for your life.

4. God's Patience with Us Is Greater Than Our Reluctance

God was patient with Moses, even when Moses doubted and tried to run from his calling. God is patient with us, too. Even when I tried to make another assignment for myself, He waited. He understands our fears and our weaknesses, and He walks with us through them. He doesn't give up on us just because we're hesitant or slow to step into our purpose. His plans for us are greater than our fears, and His patience is greater than our reluctance.

From Reluctance to Leadership: Moses's Transformation

Moses did step into his calling. He confronted Pharaoh, led the Israelites out of Egypt, and became one of the greatest leaders in the Bible. But it didn't happen because Moses suddenly became confident. It happened because Moses learned to trust God's power. God used a man who was full of fear, doubt, and excuses to perform miracles, lead a nation, and communicate directly with Him. The same God who transformed Moses is the God who calls *you*. He isn't waiting for you to feel fully prepared—He's waiting for you to trust Him.

CHAPTER 10
TRUSTING GOD'S TIMING

There's a phrase something you've heard more times than you will admit: "God's timing is perfect." And while it sounds like something easily embraced, living through it often feels like living through hell. Waiting for that breakthrough, that healing, or that long-prayed-for answer can test your patience like nothing else. It will test your relationships with people and with God. The truth is, God's timing rarely matches our time, but there's always a reason for the wait. Understanding why God's timing is different from ours, and learning to trust in His plan, is a journey of faith.

It's no secret that we live in a world of instant gratification. We want things now. The microwave society that wants to pop stuff up and in five minutes it's done. Whether it's success, relationships, or answers to our prayers—we want the answers to come in radiation timing. But God, in His wisdom, doesn't work on our schedule. His timing is based on His divine perspective, one that sees the entire picture, from beginning to end, and He knows whether or not what you waiting on or working toward—is a part of your process or plan. What looks like a delay to us could be God's preparation for something greater.

Take, the story of Abraham and Sarah. They were promised a son, but the fulfillment of that promise didn't come right away. To Abraham and Sarah, they probably felt like God had forgotten about them. But during that waiting period, God was preparing them, stretching their faith, and shaping their character. When Isaac finally arrived, it was the perfect time—not a moment too soon or too late.

God sees what we don't—He knows when we're truly ready for the next step. Get this, He knows what's best for us even when we don't understand. It's hard to accept, but His delays are not denials; they are part of His perfect plan. I really want you to embrace this: there is a danger of rushing ahead or delaying God's plan.

Rushing ahead of God's timing can lead to heartache and consequences we never intended or expected. Abraham and Sarah's impatience led them to take matters into their own hands. Sarah suggested that Abraham have a child with her servant, Hagar. While that child, Ishmael, was born, the decision caused strife and conflict that would ripple through generations. It was a human attempt to fulfill a divine promise—and it didn't work out the way they had hoped. Still to this day, the battle of the brothers exist.

On the other hand, delaying obedience to God's timing can also be dangerous. Remember Jonah? He was called to go to Nineveh, but instead, he ran in the opposite direction. His delay didn't change God's plan nor His mind; it prolonged the inevitable, and Jonah paid a price for his disobedience and also caused what could have been destruction on the lives of those around him. You have to know that when you delay…you deny yourselves and others the protection you need during the times of working. Delaying God's timing can cause us to miss out on blessings and create unnecessary complications in our lives and in the lives of those around us.

Now, I'm not saying you shouldn't wait on God's perfect timing. There's power in waiting, and testimonies of those who have waited on God's timing show that He is always faithful. You will fall flat if I told you all of the times I had to navigate seasons of waiting. It's not easy, but I found out that if you wait on the Lord, He really will renew your strength. Learning from my very own personal experiences, has thought me God's always on time, and a few biblical stones has been my examples like Joseph, David, and Hannah.

Joseph waited years to see his dreams come true, enduring betrayal, slavery, and prison. Yet, in the end, God did just as He promised. He raised him to a position of power in Egypt. Joseph's waiting wasn't wasted—it was a time of preparation.

David was anointed king as a young man, but he didn't ascend to the throne immediately. First off, he went right back to the fields from where he was called to continue taking care of the sheep. Can you imagine God has anointed you as king, but you still have to go back to your every day peasant work in the fields? Crazy! Then David spent years on the run from King Saul, waiting for God to fulfill His promise. Those years taught David reliance on God, shaping him into a king after God's own heart.

Hannah prayed for years to have a child, enduring the pain of infertility and the taunts of her husband's other sidepiece. Now the not having a baby was one thing, but when the sidepiece keeps popping out children and God won't even give you one child… oohhh wheee, that's another altogether different rant. In due season, God came through for Hannah. When God finally gave her a son, she named him Samuel, meaning "asked of God," and dedicated him to the Lord's service. Her waiting strengthened her faith, and her son would go on to become one of Israel's greatest prophets.

In each of these stories, waiting wasn't passive—it was active, filled with faith, obedience, and trust in God's perfect timing. And even in my own story, being able to keep the faith is indeed what brought me through. God gave me stone Linda Baldwin, so I could see firsthand that sometimes I would have to go broke, broken, by myself—with no support, in the midst of learning how to forgive, in the face of my enemies, at the risk of looking stupid, but all that mattered is whether I kept the faith. Whether I allowed the measure of faith to keep me focused.

So, I know you are asking, how did you remain faithful during these seasons of waiting? Especially, since it's easy to feel discouraged, to wonder if God has forgotten us or if we've somehow missed His plan. You simply have faith in God. Faith is trusting that God is at work, even when we can't see it.

Hebrews 11:1 tells us that "faith is the substance of things hoped for, the evidence of things not seen." During the waiting season, we're called and commissioned to walk by faith, not by sight. Even when the path seems unclear, or the answer feels distant, our faith can be strengthened as we lean into God, trusting His character and His promises, and hanging on to His Word.

Faith in the waiting season means continuing to pray, worship, serving, and continuing to sow seeds. It means holding onto the hope that God's timing is perfect, even when it doesn't align with our expectations. Like Joseph, David, and Hannah, we can trust that God is using our waiting period to prepare us for what's next.

Here are a few practical ways to stay productive and spiritually aligned while waiting for God's timing:

Stay in the Word: The Bible is full of stories of people who had to wait on God. Study the examples of those who waited. Meditate on the promises of Scripture and of God. Let God's Word encourage your heart during the waiting season.

Pray for Patience and Discernment: Ask God for the patience to trust His timing and the discernment to recognize His will. Prayer keeps you connected to God's heart, even when the answers aren't present. Praying for patience and discernment can be the wonder twins that help you wait, watch, anticipate, and activate.

Serve While You Wait: Don't let waiting keep you from being active in your faith. Volunteer, serve others, and find ways to use your gifts. Often, God uses these opportunities to prepare us for what's next and to keep our minds clear of doubt. When I'm working, I'm too busy to worry. You cannot worry while you work. And you cannot work, worried. Serving cancels out the spirit of worry.

Reflect on Past Faithfulness: Remind yourself of times when God has come through for you. Reflect on His faithfulness. This reflecting will help you trust that He will come through again, in His time. He's never late.

Surround Yourself With Encouragement: Stay connected to a community of believers who can encourage and support you in the waiting room. Sometimes, the waiting season can feel lonely, but you don't have to go through it alone. You just have to know who to take to the waiting room with you. I felt that! If I'm in the waiting room at the hospital—sick, I need Scroggins there. Dude is rubbing my head, praying over me, and kissing the top of my head, and although I'm hurting, I'm not alone and I have someone not looking as though I'm faking, but supporting me in the midst of my pain. It's this encouragement that gives me the strength to wait. Because eventually, my name is going to be called. Oh that's sweet right there. You've got to wait on God like you do in that waiting room. Sooner or later, He's going to call your name. As the old folks used to sing, it won't be night always…payday is coming after a while.

In conclusion:

Waiting for God's timing is rarely easy. Yet it's always worth it. God is never late; He is never in a hurry. His timing is perfect because He is perfect, and His plans for us are for good.

Whether you're waiting for a dream to be fulfilled, for healing, or for an answer to prayer, trust that God's timing is working things out far beyond what you can see or imagine. I had to think of my books as my payment to God for every good blessing He has bestowed upon me.

Like, they weren't making the money I needed them to make. I saw other people with less books than I had winning whiles I was waiting, watching, doing good, but getting nothing in return. I had to sometimes stop following people so I wouldn't see them progressing and get jealous of what God is doing in their lives. I had to take my focus off others and put my focus solely on the God who promised that if I write the vision, make it plain, others will see it and run with it.

This all goes back to trusting God, praying, depending on Him and His will, and waiting on His perfect timing.

Stay faithful. Stay patient. And when the waiting is over, you'll see that God was with you every step of the way, preparing you for something far greater than you could have ever planned on your own. Put your trust in He who can do exceedingly, abundantly, above all you can ask or think according to the power that works in you (Ephesians 3:20)

CHAPTER 11
COMPARISON: THE ENEMY OF PURPOSE

I just touched on this but I had to run it back. It's easy to look around and feel like everyone else is ahead of you. Whether on social media, at work, or at church, we're constantly bombarded with glimpses of other people's lives—the highlight reels. Before we know it, we find ourselves comparing our journey to theirs. We begin questioning our own progress and even doubting our purpose. But comparison is not only unhelpful—it's dangerous. It steals joy, fosters insecurity, and distracts us from the unique path God has set before and plans He has for us.

There is a danger in comparing your journey to someone else's journey. Why? No two people are the same. You cannot expect their journey to be yours. You victory isn't theirs is it? So whether it's the work, journey, victory, or failures, yours is yours and theirs is theirs.

Comparison is a trap. When we fixate on how someone else's life looks—how successful, happy, put-together they seem—we lose sight of what God is doing in our own lives. Instead of trusting that

He is working things out for us, we start to feel like we're falling behind schedule. That we're not enough, or that maybe we've missed something. This mindset leads to insecurity, unbelief, and doubt.

We then start to question our worth, our calling, and even God's plan for us. When we start measuring ourselves by other people's accomplishments, instead of God's standards, we box ourselves into the same lion's den Daniel was in. When we measure ourselves to others, we put ourselves in a losing battle. We become like *Martin*—on the show, *Martin*. The episode that resembles this is when he gets in the ring with *Hitman Hearns*—he's fighting a losing battle. Why? Because *Hitman* has been fighting much longer than him and *Martin* has not been fighting at all. There will always be someone ahead of, more skilled, more accomplished, or simply, better than us in some area. But here's the truth: someone else's success doesn't diminish your own. God's plan for me or you is not in competition with anyone else's plan.

So we must be careful of our minds and the outside sources that fosters a culture of comparison. Take social media as an example. Social media is one of the biggest culprits when it comes to fostering comparison. With just a few taps, you're scrolling through a feed of perfectly curated moments—weddings, promotions, travel, family milestones—all packaged to look effortless. What you don't see is the struggle behind the scenes. People rarely post all of the failures or failed relationships they go through to get to the perfect photo op moment. No one rarely says, "The waiting periods almost took me out." They never say, "I would have fainted, had I not seen the hand of the Lord in my home." All right David, come through with that good old Psalm 27:13-14, and minister to us.

David says, "I had fainted, unless I had believed to see the goodness of the Lord in the land of the living. Wait on the Lord: be of good courage, and he shall strengthen thine heart: wait, I say, on the Lord."

Dear hearts, it can't get no deeper than that!

Even when we know that social media doesn't tell the whole story, it's still hard not to feel like we're missing out or falling short. We start comparing our behind-the-scenes to someone else's highlight reel, and it feeds insecurity. Sometimes, you have to fast from the things that harbors comparison. Remember: social media is a filtered reality. It's not a reflection of someone's entire journey, and it's definitely not a standard for measuring your own progress.

I've struggled with comparison more times than I'd like to admit. There have been seasons when I've looked at others' lives and felt like I wasn't measuring up. I'd see friends who were advancing in their writing careers, jobs, building families, or living out their callings, and it felt like I was stuck. It wasn't that I didn't believe God had a plan for me—I did. But it was hard not to compare my timing and progress to theirs.

It felt like I was stuck in the *Flintstone* ages and some of them were living a *Jetson's* type of life. I saw their marriages flourishing and then started to compare the fact that I was on husband number two. It was rough at times.

What I had to learn, and what I'm still learning, is that comparison is a thief. It steals your peace, joy, and blinds you to the blessings right in front of you. Instead of focusing on the path God has for you, you end up distracted, doubting, and discouraged. You end up relishing in someone else's expected in and not anticipating your own.

I had to realize that my journey was never meant to look like anyone else's. God has a unique plan for each of us, and when we compare, we're essentially telling God that His timing isn't good enough. That His plan is not the plan we desire. That His will means nothing to us, but yet we pray, 'Your will be done on earth as it is in heaven.' With or without your permission, God's will has to be done.

Since Holy Spirit brought David in the mix, let's explore him a little deeper.

One of the clearest examples of the danger of comparison in the Bible is the story of King Saul and David. In 1 Samuel 18:7-9, after David had defeated Goliath, the people sang a song that praised David's victory, saying, "Saul has slain his thousands, and David his tens of thousands." There it is. Instead of celebrating the fact that David had won a great victory for Israel, Saul became consumed with jealousy. He couldn't handle the fact that David was being praised more than him.

Saul's comparison of himself to David led him down a dark path of insecurity, jealousy, and eventually, disobedience to God. His focus shifted from leading the nation of Israel to obsessing over and blocking David's success. He became a mad man whose energy was consumed with bringing a man down. What started as comparison grew into bitterness, and it distracted him from his God-given purpose as king.

This story is a powerful reminder that when we focus on someone else's journey, we can lose sight of our own. Saul's jealousy kept him from seeing the bigger picture—God was using both him and David for His purposes, but in different ways. Saul's fixation on comparison ultimately cost him his peace and his kingship. And eventually, he committed suicide. Who wants to give all of your energy toward causing someone else's demise? And whether you try to stop of block them, nothing you do will work if God is for them.

Kind souls, take your eyes off other people and put them on you.

So I'm throwing this in. When I started writing, all of the authors I watched were only putting out one book a year. I compared myself to them and said, "I'll do the same thing." Well, one day, I found myself listening to a woman online. She said, "You can't compare yourself to someone else. They may just have the faith to write one book. My faith is greater than that."

It was like the dig of my heart. I had so many books just sitting on my computer. I was just waiting on the next year to come around. After that, I started asking God to help me release according to my faith. In one summer, I released a book a week. After that, my social media followers went up. My readership expanded. My money started going up, and people were now watching me. Yet, I still say to some of them, "Don't watch me. I'm moving according to the faith that God has allotted me. Move at your own faith level." You have to stay focused on your own journey. Danyelle, how do we resist the temptation to compare ourselves to others? How do we stay focused on the unique path God has for us?

Know Your Identity in Christ: The first step to overcoming comparison is to be rooted in your identity as a child of God. Your worth isn't determined by your accomplishments. Nor is it determined by how you measure up to others. It's simply found in who you are in Christ. When you know who you are in Him, you can stop seeking validation from others.

Celebrate Others' Successes: One of the best ways to combat comparison is to genuinely celebrate others' successes. Instead of feeling threatened by someone else's progress, choose to rejoice with them. When we can celebrate others, it shifts our focus from competition to gratitude, and it reminds us that there's enough room for everyone to fulfill their purpose.

Practice Gratitude: Gratitude is a powerful antidote to

comparison. When you start focusing on what God has already done in your life, it shifts your perspective and causes you to actively see His movement in your life. Make it a habit to thank God for where you are, even if it's not where you want to be yet.

Limit Your Social Media Intake: If social media is a major trigger for comparison, it might be the perfect time to set some boundaries or fast off of social media. Take breaks from scrolling, unfollow accounts that stir up envy or insecurity, and focus on using social media in a way that uplifts you rather than brings you down.

Trust God's Timing: Comparison often stems from feeling like we're falling behind, but God's timing for your life is perfect. Trust that He is working things out for your good. He's the perfect behind the scenes type of guy. He writes, finds the characters, creates the plot, and always make the people who follow His plans, life end in an HEA—Happily Ever After. Remember that your path and story is uniquely yours, and it's unfolding exactly as it should. I had to learn how to be content.

Paul said it like this: *"Not that I speak in respect of want: for I have learned, in whatsoever state I am, therewith to be content (Philippians 4:11)."*

Learning to be content with where God has placed you is a process, but it's essential for finding peace. Contentment doesn't mean settling or giving up on your dreams—it means trusting that God is at work in your life. It's taking every step in the right direction. Trusting where your feet are is where they are supposed to be. Trusting that each of your steps are ordered by the Lord. Waiting and watching to receive the delights from your set path.

Contentment is everything and it's easy to get it. Sometimes it takes looking at someone who is worse off than you. I found if nothing else pulls me into a place of gratefulness and blocks the spirit of comparison off of this chick, it's that. God will give me a swift kick in the brain and at that point, gratefulness becomes my lot.

Start by practicing gratitude daily. Reflect on the ways God has blessed you and how far He has brought you. It's easy to get caught up in what you don't have, but when you focus on what you do have, you'll see that God has been faithful all along. You'll see that He has never forgotten about you and yours. You'll see that His mercy really has been everlasting, and that His truth is still enduring throughout your families generations.

Contentment also grows when you stop comparing your journey to others. You have to start embracing the unique purpose God has for you. Your calling, your gifts, and your timing are all tailored specifically to you. Just as yours won't work for me, mine won't work for you. And it's like I tell my children... There are a lot of Danyelle's or Danielle's on the earth. But Danielle S. isn't me, and Danyelle S. isn't her. We both are D. S's, we both are writers, our first name are both Danyelle/Danielle, we both have a last name that starts with the letter "S", but we both are on our own separate journey. I honor what the Lord has done in her career. But I don't envy what He's done for her. I simply trust that whatever He's doing for me will cause the world to see that God blesses the girls whose name is Danyelle/Danielle. Trust that God is writing your story, and it's a story worth waiting for.

Always remember....

Comparison is the enemy of purpose. It distracts us from the unique path God has set for us. When we focus on others' lives, we lose sight of our own calling, and we miss the beauty and blessings of what God is doing in our lives. But when we trust His timing, practice gratitude, and stay rooted in our own identity in Christ, we can let go of comparison and embrace the journey He has for us.

Dear Hearts, your purpose is too important to be derailed by someone else's progress. Stay focused, stay faithful, and trust that God's plan for you is unfolding exactly as it should. And by all means, stop wasting time. Procrastination is a derailment.

CHAPTER 12
PROCRASTINATION: A SILENT THIEF

Procrastination is more than just a delay; it's a silent thief that holds people back from fulfilling their purpose. Every time we choose to wait—whether it's out of fear, doubt, or the false belief that more time is always available—we are actively stepping away from the path that God has set for us. But why do we procrastinate, and how can we break free from its grip?

One of the most dangerous lies we tell ourselves is, "I'll do it tomorrow." We push aside what needs to be done today, assuming we have tomorrow or an endless amount of time. But scripture reminds us that our days are numbered (Psalm 90:12), and we don't know what tomorrow will bring (James 4:14). Procrastination isn't just about being late to complete a task; it's about missing out on the divine opportunities God places before us every day.

I understand this struggle too well. Throughout my own spiritual journey, procrastination held me back from stepping into God's calling for my life. There were moments when I felt a strong urge to serve in ministry, write, or encourage others, yet I hesitated. Whether it was fear of failure, a lack of confidence, or the comfort of staying where I was, the result was the same—delay. That delay impacted my spiritual growth, and I now realized that each time I postponed by not stepping into action, I was not only delaying my purpose but also hindering my relationship with God and allowing the lack of faith to set my course.

One specific moment stands out. I kept hearing God say, "If you read my Word, I'm going to take you places you've never been before."

Surely anyone who has even sat down and read the Bible from cover to cover knows that Old Testament can be a booger bear. I can't tell you how many times I started...."In the beginning God created the heaven and the earth...," but by the time I got to chapter ten, I was tired. All those names and generation about done took me out. So, I procrastinated.

How could He trust me to teach the Gospel to the world when it was so boring that I never got the real desire to read it? I realize this now, we only share the things we truly understand and the things we know. God could not trust me to share His Word when I barely wanted to read it.

Well, thanks be unto God, someone created audiobooks. All I needed was someone to read it for me. It became so interesting. Procrastination—is simply a tool presented by the devil. If he can derail you from the plan, then he can accomplish his goals: to kill, steal, and destroy.

Let's explore: The Parable of the Talents

The Bible offers a powerful lesson about procrastination in the Parable of the Talents (Matthew 25:14-30). In this story, a master entrusts his servants with talents (a form of money), expecting them to use and multiply what they've been given. Two of the servants take immediate action and double their master's investment. But the third servant, out of fear and hesitation, buries his talent in the ground, returning it without any increase.

This parable teaches us the dangers of inaction. The third servant didn't lose the talent, but his lack of initiative was condemned. You mean to tell me God doesn't want us to play it safe? Nope! Not even if we scared. Procrastination in our spiritual lives is similar—we may not lose what God has given us, but by delaying, we miss the opportunity to multiply our gifts and serve His kingdom. God calls us to be proactive, not passive, with the time, talents, and opportunities He provides.

Breaking the Cycle of Procrastination

1. **Identify the Root Cause of Procrastination** Often, procrastination stems from fear—fear of failure, fear of inadequacy, or even fear of success. Take time to identify what is truly holding you back; which one of these is affecting you. Once you pinpoint the source, you can address it directly through prayer, reflection, and counsel.
2. **Set Small, Faith-Based Goals** One of the most prevalent reasons people procrastinate is feeling overwhelmed by the size of the task ahead. Your vision is too big and it over powers your money or wisdom. Well, instead of embracing fear over the over-all vision, break it down into smaller, manageable steps. Setting small, faith-based goals helps you maintain momentum. For example, if God has called you to start a ministry, begin by serving in a smaller role at your church or community. Teach Sunday school. If you can keep a child's attention, you can keep anyone's attention. By taking that first step, you will feel encouraged.

3. **Create Accountability** Share your goals with someone you trust—a friend, mentor, or pastor. Allow them to hold you accountable for the steps you plan. When someone else is checking in on your progress, it becomes harder to make excuses or delay action. Now, you need some folks who don't play. They will put a foot on your neck so heavy, you can't help but move. For this, God sent me a woman named, Josephine Brown. When I tell you sometimes I want to cut her little foot off. Yet, I know God sent her to keep me focused.
4. **Embrace God's Timing** We must remember that procrastination delays God's plans for our lives, but rushing ahead of His timing is equally detrimental. Spend time in prayer to discern His timing for your steps, and ask for the wisdom and courage to act when He says, "Go." Ask the Lord to give you the spirit of Issachar's sons who understood the times and seasons (1 Chronicles 12:32).
5. **Take Immediate Action** The best way to break the cycle of procrastination is to take action, no matter how small. Whether it's sending that email, making that phone call, or starting that project you've been putting off, do something today. The more you act, the easier it becomes to keep moving forward.

God has placed a unique calling on each of our lives, and procrastination is one of the enemy's tools to keep us from fulfilling it. Every moment we delay, we are stolen from. Let's not be like the servant who buried his talent, but instead, let's take action with what God has entrusted to us, moving forward with faith and purpose, starting today.

CHAPTER 13
DISCERNING YOUR DIVINE ASSIGNMENT

Each of us is created with a divine purpose—a specific assignment that only we can fulfill. Discerning that assignment can feel overwhelming. Seeking the pieces that completes the puzzle can be challenging, but God has equipped us with the tools, pieces, picture, and the guidance we need to uncover it. Understanding your unique calling isn't just about figuring out what you want to do in life. No, it's not. It's about discovering the deeper mission God has written into your soul.

The first step in discerning your divine assignment is recognizing that you have one. God has placed within each of us gifts, talents, and passions that align with His plans and His assignment for us. In Ephesians 2:10, we're reminded that we are God's handiwork, created in Christ to do good works which He has already prepared in advance for us to do. Your calling is not a mystery to God or a secret being kept from us. God desires for you to know it too.

But how do you uncover this calling? Start by reflecting on the areas in your life where you feel a deep sense of fulfillment and joy.

What are the skills that come naturally to you?
What causes or opportunities stir up passion in your heart?
What makes you smile the brightest?
What makes you feel the most fulfilled?

God often reveals our assignments through these inclinations, using them to guide us toward the work we are meant to do. For all four of these questions, I have not one answer but two: Preaching and Writing.

Take a moment to consider the unique gifts and passions God has placed within you. These are not random pieces of your fabric. These things are intentionally woven into the fabric of your being for His purpose. The things you're passionate about are clues to your divine assignment. Maybe it's a love for teaching, serving, or encouraging others. Or perhaps you have a talent for creating, leading, or problem-solving. These gifts are meant to glorify God and serve others.

Reflecting on your natural abilities and interests can help illuminate your path. God uses our strengths to fulfill His purposes. What may seem ordinary and simple to you could be the key to unlocking extraordinary impact for your life and others.

Guiding Questions and Self-Reflection

To help you discern your calling, ask yourself these reflective questions:

What activities bring me the most joy and fulfillment?
What skills or talents come naturally to me?
What do others often come to me for advice or help with?
What causes or problems in the world stir up passion or frustration within me?

Where have I seen God's hand moving in my life, opening doors or providing opportunities?

When I pray about my future, what thoughts or visions does God consistently place on my heart?

Taking the time to answer these questions can give you a clarity and a clearer picture of the unique path God has set before you.

Like many of you, I spent years trying to figure out what my purpose was. I explored various career paths, sought validation in success, and even took on jobs that seemed like they would provide a sense of fulfillment. But deep down, I knew there was more—something God was calling me to that I hadn't yet allowed myself to think I could do.

It wasn't until I was locked in a jail cell in Henderson, Texas that I realized preaching and teaching the Gospel is what I am called to do. I got walked into the cell, I told the women, "Don't stop talking now." Then I laid down against a wall. When I woke up, there was a lady sitting over me in a chair.

At first, I got angry. Why is she in my space, sitting over me? Then she said, "What do I need to do to be saved?" I said, "Why would you ask me that?" She said, "Something told me you would know."

I know it wasn't something. More like someone. And I knew the someone was the Holy Spirit. He had led her to ask me what I knew in my heart.

I immediately asked her to get a Bible. I lead her through what I learned was the Romans Road To Salvation. By the time I finished, I had every ear in the room except for one who refused to leave her bed. For four days, I held revival. I even built a choir. The girl who couldn't hold a note gave parts and made a choir. Knowledge that came from another stone in my life, my aunt Diane Kimble Walls Jenkins.

I'd watch her put choirs together and teach singing as if it were her only assignment. She could keep me on key when no one else could. She encouraged me to sing and knew I couldn't hold a note. Now, I sing unto the Lord so earth's note isn't my goal...heaven's heart is.

I left jail knowing I had no choice but preach the Gospel. And last thing, God had a missionary to come in after day two, and she confirmed everything I had taught. The women were saying, "She's a real prophet." I barely saw myself as a preacher and now they were calling me prophet. I embraced their tag and when God told me to speak, I spake. God started letting those women out of that jail one by one.

And the Lord sent a prophet who saw my name in the newspaper to come bail me out of jail. Pastor K. D. Davis from Corsicana Texas, a man I'd never heard of. A man I'd never seen a day in my life became the ram caught in the thickets to bring me out and take me home.

There were moments of uncertainty and fear, but as I trusted God and stepped out in faith, then doors began to open. The opportunities that aligned with my gifts and passions felt natural, and I knew I was walking in God's will. Discerning your assignment may take time, but if you trust God's guidance, He will reveal it to you in His perfect timing.

The Role of the Holy Spirit in Revealing Your Purpose

As believers, we are not left to figure out our divine assignment alone. The Holy Spirit is our guide, leading us into all truth and revealing God's will for our lives. In John 16:13, Jesus promised that the Spirit of truth would guide us into all truth. This includes the truth of who God is, the truth of who we are in Christ, and the specific calling God has placed on our lives.

When you invite the Holy Spirit into your discernment process,

He illuminates the path you are meant to take. He gives clarity where there is confusion. He brings peace where there is uncertainty. He shuts the mouths of the naysayers. He also lends boldness to step into your assignment. When you rely upon the Holy Spirit to reveal your purpose, He ensures that you are walking according to God's will and not your own desires. This is my favorite right here: He anoints you for the task. You might can fake on my calling, but you can never deny or fake on the anointing.

Strategies to Clarify Your Assignment

Prayer and meditation help you to spend intentional time in prayer, asking God to reveal His plan for your life. Meditation on scripture and listening to God's voice can bring clarity to the areas where He is calling you. Focus on verses that remind you of God's purpose, such as Jeremiah 29:11, and ask Him to guide you as you seek your assignment.

Journaling your thoughts and experiences is another powerful way to process your thoughts. Reflect on your journey through writing and notice patterns in how God has been moving in your life. Write down the prayers you've prayed, the opportunities that have arisen, and the passions that continue to stir in your heart.

Seek community support by surrounding yourself with a community of believers who can offer encouragement, wisdom, and accountability. Often God will speak through others to confirm your calling. He will expose some secret things to them, in order for you to tune in to what they are saying to you. I cannot tell you how many times I heard: "Girl, God is going to use you." Or, "There's a calling on your life." Trusted mentors, pastors, and friends can provide valuable insights into the gifts they see in you and the areas where God may be leading you.

One of my greatest mentors, Dr. Murphy Hunt, said this to me: "Always study to show yourself approved. Men cannot deny the assignment on your life when they hear God's Word coming from your lips. Don't ever stop reading."

And because of that stone, I have a library full of books that I continue to read. Some, I have read only once. Some, I've skimmed through. But others like the ones he assigned: Watchmen Nee, C. S. Lewis Collection, and S. D. Gordon, I've read over and over again.

Stepping out on faith is sometimes the best way to discern your assignment. Faith helps you to take action. If you feel a nudge toward a specific area, take a small step of faith. Whether it's volunteering in a ministry, starting a new project, or mentoring someone, taking action can bring clarity to your calling.

Discerning your divine assignment is a journey of faith, trust, and reflection. God has placed a unique calling on your life, and as you seek Him, He will guide you toward it. Recognizing the gifts and passions He's given you, relying on the Holy Spirit, and taking practical steps, can move you confidently in the direction of your calling. Embrace the process, trust God's timing, and know that you were created for a purpose beyond what you can imagine.

CHAPTER 14

SURROUNDING YOURSELF WITH
THE RIGHT PEOPLE

The people we choose to surround ourselves with have a significant impact on our lives. Whether it's in our pursuit of purpose or happiness, those who we chose to place in our circles has the first saw in the matters of our hearts. The Bible is full of examples of how relationships can either propel us toward God's calling or pull us away from it. Godly relationships are more than just friendships—they are partnerships in faith. They can help us grow, stay accountable, and remain focused on our divine assignment. Or they can pull us away from God, plant seeds of doubt and discontentment, or cause us to be hated. Either way, you chose.

Your environment also plays a critical role in shaping your mindset, behavior, and spiritual growth. Proverbs 13:20 tells us, "Walk with the wise and become wise, for a companion of fools suffers harm." This verse reminds us that the company we keep can either help us advance in wisdom or lead us into harm. When you are surrounded by people who challenge, inspire, and encourage you, it becomes easier to stay on task. It's easier to meet the new day with success in mind.

On the other hand, toxic relationships can drain your energy, pull you away from God's will, and hinder your progress. Toxic relationships can make you hide from people and drown yourself in sorrow. Whether it's a relationships that feeds doubt, foster negativity, or tempt you to compromise your values, the wrong associations can block you from stepping into what God has called you to do.

The right community of people can be a source of immense strength. If you are lacking in faith, find you someone with crazy faith the late Linda Baldwin had. If you are struggling to get understanding—find someone who knows the Word like Superintendent David Gatlin Sr. or Dr. Murphy Hunt did. If you are struggling to stay on beat—find you someone who had an ear for notes like Diane Kimble Walls Jenkins had. Whatever you lack, there is someone near you that have what you need in the mouth or belly. You just have to have enough faith to find them and enough courage to foster that relationship.

Finding and building relationships with those who share your values, respect your calling, and challenge you to grow is essential for staying on top of the game and completing your course. These people don't just support you; they hold you accountable, help you see the bigger picture, help you grow, and they help you pray when you're tempted to give up.

Look for individuals who are spiritually grounded, passionate about the faith, and committed to their own God-given purpose. Like mindedness is not just a vibe, it's a must when it comes to those around you. This is what helps me the most…surrounding myself with people who are pursuing their own divine assignments. To me, they naturally challenge me to stay focused on my assignment. These relationships should foster spiritual growth, encouragement, and accountability.

My Experiences with Mentorship and Support Systems

In my own journey, I've been blessed with mentors and support systems that have guided me through critical moments of growth and decision-making. There have been times when I was unsure of my next steps. Then just when I feel depleted, God will send a mentor in with the wisdom and encouragement I needed to keep me grounded.

One of the most significant lessons I've learned is the importance of vulnerability in relationships. I struggled to open up to others about my challenges, fears, and uncertainties. Basically, because I didn't want to be judged. However, when you find a good mentor, you want to be naked before them. You want them to know the whole truth and nothing but the truth. This nakedness before them can bring you to confession that ultimately frees you. Mentorship, played a pivotal role in shaping my perspective and sharpening my focus on God's plans for my life.

Having someone who has walked a similar path can provide not only insight but also practical advice and spiritual encouragement when you need it most. The support systems I've built have been foundational to my growth. I can't tell you how much they helped me become more confident in my calling.

Ruth and Naomi—The Power of Supportive Relationships

The story of Ruth and Naomi (Ruth 1:16-18) is a beautiful example of how a supportive relationship can change the course of our lives. After the death of their husbands, Naomi urged her daughters-in-law to return to their families. While Orpah complied, Ruth chose to stay with Naomi, saying, "Where you go I will go, and where you stay I will stay. Your people will be my people and your God my God."

Ruth's commitment to Naomi was more than just loyalty; it was an alignment of purpose. By staying with Naomi, Ruth placed herself in a position to fulfill God's plan for her life. Her relationship with Naomi led her to Boaz. Yes, the rich cousin who became her husband. Then eventually, Ruth became the great-grandmother of King David, through whose lineage Jesus would be born. See, when you stay on the track of destiny, you'll meet up with some blessings that will blow your mind. All these many years later, women are still trying to happen up on a man like Ruth's Boaz.

This story shows the power of having the right people in your life and by your side. When you align yourself with individuals who are pursuing God's will, your own path becomes clearer, and God's plans for your life begin to unfold in powerful ways right before your eyes.

Fostering Healthy, Purpose-Driven Relationships

1. **Pray for Discernment** Before building new relationships or deepening existing ones, ask God for discernment. Pray for wisdom to recognize which relationships are helping you grow and which are hindering your progress. I have a friend in my circle who says, "She prayed for me." Technically, I wasn't praying for her, but when she presented herself, I realized God was giving me another sister.
2. **Seek Relationships That Encourage Growth** Surround yourself with people who push you to be better—spiritually, mentally, and emotionally. Look for those who aren't afraid to challenge you when you need it. I can't imagine being a star and no one tells me when I'm wrong. I'd never want you in my circle if you can't rebuke me. If you see me going to the left and you allow

it, when I come to my senses, I'm cutting you off. Why? Because if you let me go into the mud and you see me, and don't stop me…I can do dirt-dirt by myself.

3. **Be Intentional About Community** Healthy relationships don't just happen; they require effort. Be intentional about seeking out faith-based communities where you can build strong, supportive relationships. Your church should foster healthy relationships for you. If you can't find a good friend at church, try a Bible study group, or even a small group of like-minded friends who share your values and goals. We all need someone in our lives to support, encourage, rebuke, and restore us, and sometimes you have to find what you need when it doesn't come looking for you.

4. **Offer the Same Support You Seek** Relationships are a two-way street. If you want to have a community of people who uplift and challenge you, make sure you're doing the same for others. Be the same source of encouragement, wisdom, energy, and accountability to those in your life. That doesn't mean you have to be their garbage can. However, if they spitting out junk, hold the garbage can in front of them to catch the mess they talking. Bag it, tie the bag, and right before their very eyes, take out the trash.

5. **Let Go of Relationships That Hinder Your Growth** While it's important to foster healthy relationships, it's equally important to let go of relationships that are toxic or that pull you away from God's purpose. This is one of the most difficult things, especially when those relationships have been long-standing. Two things God's people hate to do is move and let go. You talking about

shedding some tears. But there will come a time in your life when both is required in order to stay on task with the vision.

Letting go doesn't mean cutting people out of your life harshly. It means setting boundaries that protect your spiritual health and align your relationships with your divine assignment. It may be that you only talk to them via phone once a week instead of every day. It may mean leaving them at home instead of taking them on your trips. As much as you love them, the love doesn't stop. You have to learn how to love them from a distance. Sometimes stepping away from certain relationships is necessary for your growth and for the fulfillment of God's plan in your life.

Remember, that we all have some ways about ourselves that others may not like. I know I do. I'm such a force and I can over power you if you aren't sound. But yet, I still have flaws. I'm still sick just like you. We go to God's church to get checkups. We also go to get a dose of medication (The Word) which has the power to heal us. So it's not that you think you are better than someone else. It's simply that you can do better without them in your company. Harsh, but you shall know the truth and the truth will make you free.

Conclusion: Building Relationships That Support Your Divine Assignment

The relationships you build are a crucial part of your spiritual journey. Surrounding yourself with the right people—those who challenge, encourage, and walk alongside you in faith—can help you stay focused on your divine assignment. Like Ruth and Naomi, these relationships can open doors and align you with God's greater plan. I often tell the people who travel with me in ministry,

"We have to be so air-tight that the devil will have no room to get in our camp."

It's almost like we are little children. I don't do for one unless I'm doing for all three. I bless them each according to what my heart is led to give. I make sure that we stay on one accord. This is what friendship is about. I nip the mess in the bud before it takes root. Simply because I need people that are going to help me in ministry not hinder me with mess.

As you move forward, be intentional in seeking godly community, foster relationships that uplift your spirit, and let go of those that no longer serve your growth. In doing so, you'll find the support and encouragement you need to walk confidently in your calling.

CHAPTER 15
WALKING BOLDLY IN YOUR DESTINY

Walking in your God-given purpose requires more than just understanding your assignment—it requires boldness, confidence, and faith to step into it fully. It takes patience and prayer, to stick with it. It takes obedience and fasting, to not let it go. God has called each of us to fulfill a unique role in His kingdom, but fulfilling that role means embracing it with a heart of courage, a tenacity of relentlessness, and a divine determination that even when fear and uncertainty try to stand in the way, you won't falter.

Owning your assignment is about more than just acknowledging that you have a purpose; it's about stepping forward with authority, knowing that God has equipped you for this journey. I have a friend who was called into the ministry. One man, the fear of moving, and the uncertainties of life was able to stop her from going forward. I'm so grateful I embraced who I am before one more man could tell me differently.

Confidence in your calling allows you to face obstacles, doubts, and challenges head-on, trusting that you are walking in the path He has prepared for you. I trust and believe I am who I am to the point that I'm willing to suffer the hardship of stripes. See, those who do wrong and know to do right will be whooped with many stripes. I've had enough whoopings on earth to ever want one in heaven. So I vowed to operate solely in the assignment that God has called me to, but it takes courage.

Breaking Through Fear: Living Fearlessly and Boldly

Fear is one of the greatest barriers to walking boldly in your destiny. Whether it's the fear of failure, rejection, or the unknown, fear can paralyze us and keep us from fully embracing the life God has planned. But God hasn't given us a spirit of fear, but of power, love, and a sound mind (2 Timothy 1:7). Overcoming fear is essential to living out your calling.

Here are some practical tips for living fearlessly:

1. **Recognize the Source of Fear** Understand that fear often doesn't come from God. While fear can feel real, it is usually a tactic of the enemy to keep you from stepping into your destiny. I wrote about it in my book *40 Days of Healing,* as a ferocious dog barking in order to keep you from getting out of a box. Once you recognize that fear is not from God, it cannot hurt you, and you have the power to bite back—you can reject it and replace it with faith.
2. **Speak God's Promises Over Your Life** Combat fear with the truth of God's Word. When fear arises, remind yourself of God's promises like the one found in Isaiah 41:10 ("Do not fear, for I am with you") and Joshua 1:9 ("Be strong and courageous"); these scriptures can empower you to move forward despite fear.

3. **Take Action in Spite of Fear** The key to breaking through fear is action. Fear loses its power the moment you take steps of faith, no matter how small. Often, you'll find that the fear you felt was an illusion, and as you move forward, God meets you with provision and strength.

Personal Empowerment: My Journey of Stepping Boldly into My Destiny

There was a time in my life when fear nearly kept me from walking in the assignment God had for me. I felt like a hostage being kept in a place of filth. Believe it or not, when we are in places God hasn't called us to, not only do we make things bad for those called to that space, it starts to stink and sour on us as well.

I was preaching not long ago and it hit me. Even when you are called by God and you go into the enemy camps, all hell breaks loose. Anytime someone holy comes into unholy spaces, you bring catastrophe on those who operate in those spaces. The Bible says those whom God loves He chastens (Hebrew 12:6-7). I still live by street codes. I don't need you coming up in New Vessels if you running from God. We don't want His wrath kindled our against us because you allowing fear to keep you from His favor.

It wasn't until I chose to push past the fear and trust in God's strength that I began to see doors open. By stepping out, even when I felt afraid, I found empowerment. God gave me the courage and clarity to walk in the path He had set before me. As I continued to act in faith, my confidence grew, and the fears that once seemed so daunting became smaller and smaller. Stepping boldly into my destiny wasn't just about courage; it was about trusting that God's plan for me was greater than my fears.

Biblical Example: Esther—Courage in the Face of Great Risk

The Bible is filled with people who showed courage, but none to me can compare to the story of Esther. As a young Jewish woman living in a foreign land, Esther was placed in a position of influence as the Queen of Persia. Yes, she was a queen. When her people were threatened with destruction, Esther was threatened with a life-changing decision: remain silent and watch her people perish, or risk her life by approaching the king to plead for their survival. Now can you imagine how afraid Esther was? Afraid to watch her people die. Afraid she could be killed. Gut wrenching fear.

In Esther 4:14, her cousin Mordecai famously tells her, "And who knows but that you have come to your royal position for such a time as this?" Mordecai's words reminded Esther that her assignment—her destiny—was not just for her own benefit but for the saving of many lives. With great courage, Esther chose to act, risking her life to fulfill her purpose. Her bravery and willingness to walk boldly in her assignment ultimately led to the salvation of her people.

Esther's story teaches us that walking in our destiny often requires great courage, especially in the face of risk. But it also reminds us that when God places us in a position, He equips us with everything we need to succeed. Esther didn't act alone—she fasted, prayed, and relied on God's strength to guide her. We must rely on God as we step into our own assignments, knowing that He is with us every step of the way.

Taking Ownership of Your Calling Today

1. **Acknowledge and Embrace Your Assignment** The first step in walking boldly in your destiny is to accept your calling. You must confess it with your mouth and believe it in your heart that you are who God says you are.

Spend time in prayer asking God to affirm, reaffirm, and clarify the purpose He has for you. Then do whatever it takes to help you train in that purpose. For me it is still reading. I continue to study and spend time in the presence of God.

2. **Face Your Fears with Faith** Whatever fears or doubts you may have about stepping into your calling, bring them to God, and step into the ring like Martin. Talk to your fears. I tell the people at New Vessels to talk back to anything talking to them. If it's fear, tell fear you will never win when it comes to me. Start each day by declaring you will not allow fear to hold you back, and that you will walk boldly in your destiny.

3. **Take the First Step** Boldness begins with action. Faith is action. Identify one faith move you can make today toward fulfilling your purpose. It might be starting calling another pastor or preacher, writing that first page of your book, signing up for a course or college, or reaching out to a mentor. Whatever it is, take that step in faith, knowing that God will meet you there.

4. **Surround Yourself with Encouragement** Walking boldly in your destiny is not something you do alone. Surround yourself with people who will encourage, enlighten, and uplift you in your journey. Build a support system of family members, friends, mentors, and fellow believers who will hold you accountable, check you, and cheer for you.

5. **Continually Seek God's Guidance** Boldness is not about relying on your own strength but on God's guidance. As you take steps toward your destiny, continue to seek God daily through prayer and the Word. He will provide the

wisdom, courage, and opportunities you need to fulfill your purpose.

Living Fully in Your God-Given Destiny

God has placed a unique and powerful assignment on your life, and He is calling you to walk boldly in it. Fear may try to hold you back, but with God's strength, you can overcome anything. Like Esther, you were created for such a time as this. By owning your assignment, you can break through fear, and take action in faith, and you can live out your destiny fully in living color for a lasting kingdom. Don't wait any longer—your time to walk boldly in your destiny is now. You did not get this book by chance. It's your time.

CHAPTER 16

THE JOY OF FULFILLING YOUR GOD-GIVEN PURPOSE

There is fulfillment in living in alignment with God's will. There is a deep, loving, and lasting joy that comes from living in alignment with God's will. When you step into the purpose He has ordained for your life, and His promises become exposed in your life, you experience a sense of peace and fulfillment like none other.

This feeling is one that nothing else can provide. No person, money, success, sex, or job, can ever compare to the joy you feel when you are walking in your God-given assignments. This joy is not just about achieving goals or getting rewards, but it's about knowing that you are walking in step with God, fully aligned with His plans and His heart for you.

Fulfilling your God-given purpose is not without challenges, but the joy of knowing you are exactly where God wants you to be makes the journey worthwhile. When you live in alignment with God's will, you begin to see the fruit of your obedience, not only in your own life but in the lives of those around you. This is what the

Bible talks about when it presents a joy that surpasses all understanding. Knowing who you are and walking in your assignment births a joy so rooted in you that causes you to never abandon your divine assignment.

While the joy of walking in your purpose is immense and immeasurable, it's important to remember that the journey is ongoing. It doesn't stop. There will be moments of fear, doubt, seasons of waiting, and times when the path seems unclear, but you can't quit. You must remember that God calls us to walk by faith, not by sight (2 Corinthians 5:7). Faith allows us to keep our eyes on the prize, to trust in God's timing, and to have faith in His promises; even when we don't have all the answers.

Patience is also key a special key in maintaining during this journey. Fulfilling your purpose often requires time and perseverance. 'Let patience have her perfect work in you so you can be entire, complete, and lack nothing' (James 1:3-8). You may not see immediate results, but just as seeds take time to grow, so does the fruit of your calling. Trust that God is working behind the scenes, orchestrating the details of your life in ways you cannot yet see. Trust that he is making the best deals for you and that His contracts are so air tight that no one can harm you in the process of being you.

Perseverance is what sustains you when the journey gets tough. The Bible encourages us in Galatians 6:9: "Let us not become weary in doing good, for at the proper time we will reap a harvest if we do not give up." Keep pressing forward, knowing that every step you take in faith brings you closer to the fulfillment of God's promises.

When you fully embrace your God-given purpose, you will not only experience joy and fulfillment, but you also become a vessel through which God can work and use. Your life has a ripple effect, influencing and inspiring others to pursue their own divine assignments, and to trust fully in your God. Walking in your destiny is about more than just you; it's about advancing God's kingdom and leaving a lasting legacy of faith.

2 Timothy 2:20-21 Now in a large house there are not only gold and silver implements, but also *implements* of wood and of earthenware, and some *are* for honor while others *are* for dishonor. Therefore, if anyone cleanses himself from these *things*, he will be an implement for honor, sanctified, useful to the Master, prepared for every good work.

Living in your destiny is also about discovering your full potential. When you align with God's plans, He stretches you beyond what you thought was possible, and He empowers you to achieve things you never imagined and to become a vessels of honor and good works. The gifts and talents that the Lord has placed within you come alive, and you are able to accomplish the extraordinary, and all because you are walking in His strength, your destiny, and not in your own plan.

As you reach this final chapter, my prayer is that you would fully embrace the destiny God has ordained for you. Your life has meaning and purpose, and God has chosen you for a specific assignment that only you can fulfill. No one can get the job done but you. God is so waiting on you and so are your brothers and sisters in Christ who needs something to be planted and watered in their lives. Now is the time to step boldly into that calling, trusting that God has equipped you with everything you need to succeed.

Let go of any remaining doubts, fears, or hesitations. Know that God is with you. He's got you covered. He's guiding your steps and providing the strength you need to persevere. Embrace the potential He has placed within you, and walk confidently in the path He has set before you.

This journey may not always be easy, but the joy of fulfilling your God-given purpose will carry you through every challenge. As you continue forward, remember that your obedience to God is not only bringing joy to your life but also making an eternal impact. Your obedience is stretching between the heavens and the earth, and is causing some lost soul to believe in God's hands is where they want to be.

You will never be able to imagine the joy of being used by God to bring a lost sheep home. It's better than watching your team win an important game. It's better than the preacher pronouncing that you can now kiss your bride or groom. This joy is so much more than you'd ever hoped for, and it's yours.

The joy of fulfilling your God-given purpose is within reach. As you walk in alignment with His will, live with faith, patience, and perseverance, and embrace the fullness of your destiny, you will experience a life of profound meaning and lasting joy. This is the life God has called you to live—one of purpose, impact, and divine fulfillment.

So step forward with confidence. Walk boldly in your destiny, knowing that you are fulfilling the very reason you were created. God's joy and peace are yours as you live out the full potential He has ordained for you. Now is your time to embrace all that He has for you.

RESOURCES TO FURTHER YOUR UNDERSTANDING

Check out a few additional readings to help in your journey to be.

Destined To Be: Study Guide by Danyelle Scroggins

Processed For Purpose by Danyelle Scroggins

Killing Comparison: Reject the Lie You Aren't Good Enough and Live Confident in Who God Made You to Be by Nona Jones, Piper Jones

Discernment by Jane Hamon

The Purpose Driven Life: What on Earth Am I Here For? by Rick Warren

Tozer: Mystery of the Holy Spirit by A. W. Tozer

Quiet Talks on Prayer (A Timeless Classic) by S. D. Gordon

The Spiritual Man by Watchman Nee

ABOUT THE AUTHOR

Danyelle Scroggins is the Senior Pastor of New Vessels Ministries in Shreveport, Louisiana. She is the author of special books like Put It In Ink, Graced After The Pain, Evonta's Revenge, & Enduring Love. She's the wife of Pastor Reynard Scroggins and the mother of three young adults: Raiyawna, Dobrielle, and Dwight Jr.. She's privilege to be the grandmother of Emiya'rai Grace.

Danyelle loves writing inspirational stories set in Louisiana, where she lives preaching, teaching, and enjoying writing by the window. Learn all about her here www.danyellescroggins.com.

Also find her on Facebook, Twitter, and Bookbub.

- facebook.com/authordanyellescroggins
- twitter.com/pastordanyelle
- bookbub.com/profile/danyelle-scroggins
- goodreads.com/danyellescroggins

ALSO BY DANYELLE SCROGGINS

THE NONFICTION BOOKS
NOT UNTIL YOU'RE READY https://amzn.to/3T0tBdW
HIS MISTRESS OR GOD'S DAUGHTER https://amzn.to/4dwsIC
PROCESSED FOR PURPOSE https://amzn.to/3T2XdYd
40 DAYS OF HEALING https://amzn.to/4cTALrP
A BLACK GIRL'S CRY https://amzn.to/4dyLqJv

THE SUNDAY SERVICE SERIES
YOU CAN'T SLAY STUCK https://amzn.to/4fVqnCs
YOU CAN'T PRAY SCARED https://amzn.to/3TUss8b

STANDALONES
DESTINY'S DECISION https://amzn.to/3Xdg3hR
A HEART ASSIGNED https://amzn.to/3AEUoq8
MORE THAN GRATEFUL https://amzn.to/4fWNYT5
THE POWER SERIES https://amzn.to/3YXUpiS
SOMETHING DIFFERENT https://amzn.to/3YXBzIx
EVONTA'S REVENGE https://amzn.to/3MgIFjR
MORE THAN EXPECTED https://amzn.to/3yQwNlA
PUT IT IN INK https://amzn.to/3T0x1O0
MORE THAN DIAMONDS https://amzn.to/3yGv42l

NOT TOO FAR https://amzn.to/3AyPtXJ

CURVY GIRL VALENTINES

CURVES OR CUPID https://amzn.to/3X5dXPY

CURVY GIRL HOLIDAY SERIES EBOOKS

HIS FOR CHRISTMAS https://amzn.to/3YYENfa

HOPE FOR CHRISTMAS https://amzn.to/3Xe5OKe

HOME FOR CHRISTMAS https://amzn.to/3T2TFFh

HAPPY FOR CHRISTMAS https://amzn.to/4cC56uH

HELP FOR CHRISTMAS https://amzn.to/3T2RmlB

HEALED FOR CHRISTMAS https://amzn.to/4cBHiHq

HALLELUJAH FOR CHRISTMAS https://amzn.to/471Gjza

HONOR FOR CHRISTMAS https://amzn.to/4cF9itN

KATRINA JACOBS MURDER SUSPENSE SERIES

SECRET SECRET https://amzn.to/4dzEI62

DO NOT TELL https://amzn.to/4cz5oSV

IF YOU DO https://amzn.to/3MhXLpl

YOU'LL GO TO JAIL https://amzn.to/3T54KWr

THIS TIME AROUND SERIES

SWEET LOVE https://amzn.to/4fVeD2S

A HEART ASSIGNED & A HEART ASSURED https://amzn.to/4d9zKfn

www.ingramcontent.com/pod-product-compliance
Lightning Source LLC
LaVergne TN
LVHW012054070526
838201LV00083B/4721